Finishing Well

"Starting well and ending well are two entirely different matters."

FINISHING
Well

Starting? Finishing?
On the sidelines? In the race
of faith, everyone who wants to win *can*.

Mark W. Lee

Christian Publications
CAMP HILL, PENNSYLVANIA

Christian Publications
3825 Hartzdale Drive, Camp Hill, PA 17011

Faithful, biblical publishing since 1883

ISBN: 0-87509-585-2
LOC Catalog Card Number: 95-70932
© 1996 by Christian Publications
All rights reserved
Printed in the United States of America

96 97 98 99 00   5   4   3   2   1

Contents

Acknowledgments

There are several acknowledgments that must be made. My wife, Fern, is primary colleague in my work, giving unflagging support and encouragement. In good spirit she permits me to use hours for writing that could be hers and ours. Much of our more than 50 years of experience together—experience that includes improved levels of personal evaluation and development for us—is translated here. We learned about Christian maturity together. She permits the story of our lives to provide illustrations of ideas.

My secretary in San Francisco, Yvonne Cederblom, assisted during the first preparation of this manuscript as she did others of mine for 17 years. She typed each manuscript through every revision. Without her work, mine would be greatly diminished. With her assistance I completed a book manuscript annually for several years. Later, Judith Humphries Young, using emerging technologies, helped us to speed up typing and preparation of various manuscripts. During recent years, Helen D. Lee, my daughter-in-law, picked up where the others left off at the time of my retirement in 1987 from the Presidency of Simpson College in California.

I appreciate the work of a longtime friend, Keith Bailey, author himself, who edited the manuscript.

The Board of Trustees at Simpson College was supportive of my presidential administration related to 17 years in the office there, making it possible to accomplish goals in several areas important to me. My professional situation, it seems, could not have been much improved for my purposes. No one should expect more for professional independence than I have been afforded. Because this manuscript was completed after my retirement from the presidency of the college, but also after becoming the Chancellor, the venue changed, and more time became available to follow through several new lines of thought on maturity. I have become even more aware of how maturity—Christian maturity—is vital to lifetime fulfillment.

_____ *Introduction*

This book is about maturity—primarily Christian maturity. Its purpose is to discuss and affirm maturity as an ultimate ideal for Christian personal development. Several ways to achieve that objective are suggested here, and others implied. A design emerges to make practical the ideals of Christian maturity. The appeal is primarily to Christians affirming biblical orientation in beliefs.

Christian maturity is a major biblical theme. Certainly, for devout men and women, maturity ought to be identified and developed for them in biblical analysis. From Scripture people learn whatever is genuinely Christian. Even though grateful for other resources, we know the Bible is the seminal source of Christianity. From that narrative, a Christian is identified first in a spiritually defined relationship with Jesus Christ by a human being in a faith experience. For the individual Christian, other matters, of whatever sort, are related, or ought to be, to that experience. This definition is forced upon us because of the repetition of it in authoritative Scripture. With appreciation, we acquiesce.

Thoroughgoing humanists also espouse maturity as an important life objective. Their views grow out of subjective studies in which a person is almost totally a social and biological creature. Even so, many secular writers state or imply a spiritual perception in the human maturation process. This "spiritual" factor does not, for them, require a Supreme Being, at least not a personal One. Many humanists openly espouse a "secular religion" to meet human spiritual longing.

1

We discover then that whatever their philosophical orientation, serious men and women value maturity. Numerous similarities appear in comparisons between Christian maturity and standard secular forms of maturity—personal or social. Maturity belongs to persons and may also be projected into societies. It is rather widely agreed that much of personal/social upheaval relates to the lack of maturity in human conduct. Without maturity, man finds problem-solving too difficult.

Christian maturity, biblically defined, includes application of ideals leading to personal virtue and righteous conduct—an application related to enlightened understandings and controlled emotions. It includes belief in God, God who is active in the lives of men and women. A person chooses God to help in the search to become mature. God does, primarily through Scripture, communicate with man for a purpose, and man acts.

Christian maturity, although holding similarities to some concepts of the humanist, is significantly more, and, in many factors, different from naturalistic maturity. Humanistic theorists are commonly represented by mainline psychologists, sociologists and philosophers. The Christian view then is based on a concept of what a mature person is as described in the Old and New Testaments. It is unique in its conclusions.

Christian maturity is lived out in Christian experience. Time is a factor. Maturity, as the name itself implies, is never instantaneous. It takes the passage of years for a person to become fully mature. Nevertheless, the process can be speeded up. The years can be made fewer for some men and women. George Gallup, Jr. and Timothy Jones, in their book, *The Saints Among Us*, showed that saintly persons, in the current era, are likely to be 50 years of age or older, but youthful persons may readily be found who are mature. Even so, no matter how long one lives he or she will not perfect his or her life. To be mature does not mean achievement of perfection. Direction is the important matter. Is the best purpose in sight? Tendency is vital. We will not discuss saintliness in depth, although there is overlap with maturity.

What is sometimes called Christian growth ought to be equated with maturity. Unlike physical development, highly predictable, spiritual growth follows a pattern of maturation that is special but uneven for each person. There are fallbacks and plateaus. Maturity may develop rapidly or slowly. It must be lived out. And knowledge about maturity is no assurance that the informed person will act in mature ways. Learning what one ought to become and acting upon what is learned results in maturity.

It is an aphorism that conceptualization is not actualization in human behavior. Maturity eludes society. Although admired, maturity is not widely sought. Society may avoid maturity. This is illustrated in entertainments. It seems that much of the population, Christian and non-Christian, has been somewhat mesmerized by the yelling, screaming, prideful, banal, wild-eyed, electronically circuited, popular, sometimes pseudo-sophisticated entertainment celebrities and their followers.

Many celebrities make no claim to genuine sophistication. Some would disdain refinement, disdain even education in its formal or classical meaning. Most seem to have limited knowledge about religion, history, peace, hope, order, power, service, righteousness, duty, integrity and responsibility. That large shallowness does not prevent them from broadcasting their views on various subjects, serious or popular. Also, the limitation does not prevent general society from following their leads. Celebrity culture has formed much of common life.

Entertainers have much to say about how to live. Analysts commonly argue that there is little substance to celebrity observations relative to life and society, but the public seems to follow media accents. Much of what is said by some celebrities is banal, often in response to shallow questions. Remarks these men and women make about emotions are often rudimentary and self-justifying. They seldom reflect maturation.

It appears that, in numerous ways, celebrities growing older choose to be like, and appeal to, the adolescent generation. Popular beliefs and conduct are sometimes found in rebellion against elder generations and older mores. Some persons resist maturity and its invitation to responsibility by losing themselves in drugs, alcohol, cults or other distractions. As they age they talk solemnly and sometimes graphically about their youthful excesses, but too much has been lost. Modifications appear too late and are not extensive.

Society's elders often submit to the pop culture with a "what-else-can-we-do" feeling or attitude. Those who report the youth culture through the various media appear to have been "conned." They seem to take sides, sometimes by their silences, with countercultures. They desire approval from the youths. Little analysis is made that is useful. The point is that a mammoth pop culture contributes little, if anything, to maturity.

Immaturity in individuals threatens family solidarity; therefore, it threatens society. Marriages break and dissolve because emotion related to fragile romance is not permitted to grow into love to commitment. Wholesome values are commonly denigrated. Distorted values, like greed or self-centeredness, are cast in terms like "enlightened self-interest" and "acceptance."

Money has become the measure of nearly all things. The general population evaluates its worth by what it is paid, or believes that it should be paid. From the corporation president to the shortstop on the baseball team, work and human values are judged by money, lots of it. Jokes about greed are told by the greedy and are presumed to take some of the sting out of the injury greed has visited upon the human situation. As P.T. Barnum said: "Money is a severe slave master, but a good servant." The money-master complex reigns. Servanthood, important to maturity, is too demanding.

Some social injuries relate to lack of maturity. Immaturity in society denigrates generations. Humane values, even in the family, are downgraded in society. Child abuse, especially through neglect, excessive punishment and aberrant sexual contact, has become, by the last quarter of the 20th century, a national scandal in America. According to reports, abuse has become somewhat commonplace. And abused persons tend to abuse when their time comes.

Fathers and mothers, in impacted urban settings, often seem less interested in their children than their parents were in them. There are many reasons for this shift, including a broad decline in making marriage and family commitments. The general public grooms itself and uses language with less care and sophistication than formerly. Even secular analysts are concerned about the habits of children's speech that include grossness, swearing and shallow responses to life contexts. Speech reflects the level of a person's thought life.

Even "intellectuals" lose their way. College presidents have become unsure about morals and ethics on campus and sought instruction about what to do about increasing crime among students. Alcohol abuse, murder and gang rape appeared on their campuses. They seem unable to manage scandals in athletic programs. Administrators have nearly given up on the campus drug problem. They even argue that without free use of alcohol, which always leads to some abuse, they would not have many students enroll in their colleges. The modern public college cannot survive, we are told, without the free flow of alcohol—incredible! Even faculties are infected with alcoholism.

Society sometimes demotes itself as seen in the lower status of education in some communities, in the forms of "adult" degradation in semi-popular literature and other media entertainment. During the course of 50 years of professional life, I have never met more informed people than I do currently, but also have never encountered more ignorance. Test results show a lack of basic information in the general public for effectiveness in living. In nearly every public matter, we now must lower expectations. General disinterest in maturation is also seen in the near collapse of social control and law, reported most often from large urban centers.

What about the elders in society and issues of maturity? Maturity, for our purposes, is not the physical aging process. The word maturity is often used to mean change in anatomical features such as wrinkles, baldness and weight changes. Or "mature" is used to describe couples whose children have been launched as adults. Those who have retired are referred to as mature. These factors hold modest interest for us in discussing maturity.

Old age and maturity ought to be handmaidens. This combination has something to do with the time factor in the maturation process. The apostle Paul appealed to his own seniority as reason for Philemon to regard the apostle's wishes for the treatment and relief of the slave, Onesimus. Paul had instructed Titus in another letter that aged men and women ought to possess mature habits and attitudes—soberness, graveness, temperance, faith, love and patience, which is part of holiness (see Titus 2:2-3). Whatever older generations lose in esteem through decline in physical powers or social influence can be more than made up through influence generated by maturity. Some of the best books are autobiographies distilling the maturity to wisdom of the most effective older men and women.

Enlarged problems were introduced into the "baby boomer" world of change at 20th century's end. The current elder generation is significantly larger than any preceding one in the percentage of the population and has received uneven treatment from families and society. Several problems relate to such a shift in population demographics including general employment, products and services to be provided, and the retirement of a generation that is not only proportionately larger, but will live longer than any previous generation.

Issues for individuals and society, suggested above, have

not been adequately addressed, and will not be without mature reflection and action. Inadequate solutions are currently proposed. We have increased consumerism as an answer to social ills. We must use up more and more things to keep society employed. So we tend to think quantitatively rather than qualitatively. Such a society will not work well enough. Man does not have time to consume at the level he must to keep business rolling.

Immature persons often permit emotions to get out of hand. Candidates for public offices acknowledge that they play the politics of emotion in order to gain election. Partly because of television, Americans seem to have become more publicly emotional about their lives and institutions since the student movements of the 1960s. Where their personal interests are at stake, Americans are more sensitive than ever. They never were highly intellectual about political and public issues anyway.

Lack of maturity in the society may have contributed to degradation of some human liberties. Voices of criticism, hatred and frustration by the 1970s became so intense that public forums were often little more than shouting matches between audiences and individuals or panels. Even when a forum was made up of collegians, parents or senior citizens, the confrontation was often angry, loud, abusive and marked by crude language, close-mindedness and disrespect. Persons, through individual listener or general audience rudeness, were denied free speech. John Gardner believed America was seriously threatened by "unloving critics and uncritical lovers."

Further, societal problems have negatively impacted the Church. As noted in remarks from the eminent Christian theologian, Carl F. H. Henry, the Church has not made significant affirmative impact upon the general conduct and culture of society. The polls of the Gallup organization, and other groups, provide evidence for Henry's observation. (For our purposes, we do not differentiate churches relative to theology or denominational affiliation, for prob-

lems appear across the spectrum.) Society needs the modeling of Christian maturity in volume sufficiently significant
to make perceived public impact. If serious conversation
increases about personal Christian maturity, the cycle may
turn upward, at least in some important areas like family
integrity.

We do not choose to do what many have done—look for
escape or peace in the occult, or sects, or drugs or dropping
out. Escapism is immature conduct. We look for maturity
in persons who will improve themselves and the institutions to which they belong. Institutions are strengthened
primarily by improving the persons in them. Systems succeed or fail as persons cause them to succeed or fail. Fault
is not likely found so much in systems or institutions as in
ourselves.

Serious observers are aware of the impotence of individuals in society, a society lurching along under bursts of energy
generating from large forces—governments, politics, education, economics, science, entertainment, technology, religion
and the like. Who can deny the impotency of the individual?
He feels about as important as "one more quart of water flow-
ing over mighty Niagara." A person can at least do wonders
for himself. He may do much as well for the few others
around him, especially the members of his family.

To gain control of my life; to become the best person I
can become; to cope constructively with whatever it is that
persons and society deal out to me; to assist others in the
search for meaning and direction for themselves; and, to
contribute to the kingdom of God—mean that I have won
the high objectives of my existence. Perhaps, in winning
these goals, I moderate some negative forces.

The development of Christian maturity means that one
is moving upward, elevating to higher levels of personal
growth, taking on realistic viewpoints and learning how to
feel, think and act responsibly. Personal wisdom accumu-
lates. It grows. Each individual gains understanding. Comfort with life is added—a benefit of maturity. That pleasure

creates some peace. It is possible to be satisfied, as it was for Abraham who "died in a ripe old age, an old man and satisfied with life" (Genesis 25:8, NASB).

The one factor that characterizes active and high achievers, respected by the world, is Mission. Whether the apostle Paul, Martin Luther, David Livingstone, Florence Nightingale, Mother Teresa, Admiral Rickover, or President Washington, Lincoln, the Roosevelts or others from a thousand fields, the concept of Mission in each is the common factor. These persons were unlike each other in many ways, but all confessed to Mission in their lives even though each Mission varied.

Mission is partly related to vision. Vision precedes. My life and character are not expanding for good until my vision expands about what a person can become. In that expansion, I become more (perhaps greater) than I was at a lower elevation, increasing my awareness of who I am, and discovering where I most effectively fit in.

By way of review—this book is an attempt to find what Christian maturity is, how to gain it and to suggest what it feels like when one has developed his or her own full and responsible Christian personhood. This does not directly relate to physical maturity, but maturity in other areas—emotions, thoughts, attitudes, conduct (specifically including moral actions) and relationships.

As is nearly always the case when a substantive subject emerges for consideration, there is more to be treated than the serious student believed there was at the outset of his or her investigation. One feels incompetent to treat it fully, and sometimes despairs that even if he or she is sound in reporting his or her studies and meditation, it will not make any difference. But hope springs eternal. This writing is at least a run at explaining a vital issue—*What is maturity, Christian maturity?*

Mark W. Lee
May 14, 1995

Chapter 1

Signals for Winning

Do you not know that in a race all the runners run, but only one gets the prize? Run in such a way as to get the prize. (1 Corinthians 9:24)

I press on toward the goal to win the prize for which God has called me heavenward in Christ Jesus. (Philippians 3:14)

Similarly, if anyone competes as an athlete, he does not receive the victor's crown unless he competes according to the rules. (2 Timothy 2:5)

The apostle Paul may have been something of a sports buff. Using athletic word pictures as he did, he presumed that his readers shared his knowledge about competitive games. His metaphors came from wrestling, boxing and racing—events central to the Olympic games, popular long before the first century of the Christian era in which he wrote. Although all of Paul's references to athletic competition were positive, the apostle did not imply approval or disapproval of the actual

11

games. Either way, athletics conveniently provided him with a useful rhetorical device.

We may be reluctant to apply the spiritual meanings the apostle developed to modern professional sports. The intense, sometimes crass, commercialism of modern athletes and sports managers does not permit easy parallel to the Pauline reference in which a garland is cited as sufficient reward for winning. It was from this ideal of winning against tough competition, playing strictly by rules, that the apostle drew his lesson. The fact that some athletic competitions violate the ideals of the game does not diminish the lesson.

We know that commercialism ultimately interfered with the ancient Olympics, contributing to their decline. Amateur athletics were denigrated as both promoters and athletes became driven more by profit than by the satisfaction of winning. The ideals of amateur athletics eroded for the ancient Greeks and Romans, as they have for America in the 20th century. But in his analogy, the apostle assumed winning ideals that were not self-aggrandizing. One tried to win by doing his best, and for no other reason except to win. Recognition was important, but that recognition was simple and not a matter of personal profit. Biblical metaphors of sporting events are to be understood in the context of ideal competition.

In that admirable light, where winning fairly was the main thing and financial profit meant almost nothing, the Apostle used forceful athletic metaphors. In First Corinthians 9, Paul wrote about footracing and boxing, revealing his strong opinions about winning. By Paul's reasoning, when an athlete chooses to participate, he means to win; if he does not mean to win, he will not run his best race.

The good athlete does not run in order to defeat others but rather to achieve his own personal best. Winning is its own appropriate motivation. Athletes who enter competitive events do not do so for the purposes of improving health and body tone—other activities are better for body building. They enter competitive sports because they want to win. To run well, the racer follows a regimen for achieving personal and physical discipline. Discipline is necessary for winning, because opponents are also disciplined. To win, an athlete must at least match the effort of his best adversary.

The thing that sets the spiritual contest apart from the competitive sports Paul addressed, however, is that in the spiritual race, any Christian may compete—and win—if he or she chooses to do so. There is a magnificent mystery here—everyone can win; no one has to lose.

The highly motivated apostle Paul ran the spiritual race as though he was in strong competition; he was careful to avoid stumbling because he wanted to win. Likewise, when Paul practiced spiritual boxing, he boxed against real foes; he was not shadowboxing. To succeed in his purpose he maintained his conditioning, forcing himself to respond to his own will rather than letting his will be controlled by carnal distractions. He knew that the carnal will is "out of shape" and might disqualify him from the race.

Like Paul, contemporary scholars have also compared life to sports. Emory University professor Brad Shore, an expert on behavior, has won acclaim for his research on the sociological aspects of sports in society. Shore argues that baseball represents the idea that working hard brings reward, that goals can be achieved and that people in authority are there to keep things fair.[1]

The matter of relating the lessons of sports to life is a continuing saga. During 1995, Don Shula, for decades the coach of the National Football League's Miami Dolphins, devoted much of his off-season time to motivational programs with business people. His "game plan" was based on the acrostic COACH: Conviction-driven (never compromise your beliefs); Overlearning (practice until it is perfect); Audible ready (know when to change); Consistency (respond predictably to performance); and Honesty-based (walk your talk).[2]

Even from children's games we can learn lessons. As

someone has said, "Hopscotch is chock-full of philosophy." As we grow older we tend to seek more sophisticated methods than deciphering from games and simple experiences. Even so, theologians have used hopscotch to teach theological truth. Why not? Jesus used sparrows, wheat seed, water and bread.

Wisdom develops from reflecting about everyday life, and then applying what is learned in constructive ways. Wisdom derives from evaluated experience applied to current and future events. A wise person evaluates in order to learn to function more effectively.

Having this perspective on everyday life, we realize that there are more special moments for us than we had at first believed. Special, life-changing events do not require profoundly articulated words, dramatic environments or elaborate and creative preparations. We tend to forget that ordinary persons entertain angels unawares. Parents, friends and mentors often unknowingly and without publicity make large and lasting contributions to us.

For me, one of these friends was Coach William "Bill" Scheidt. Bill Scheidt was a physical education instructor and head track coach at West High School in Akron, Ohio, where I was a student during the late 1930s. He was a rugged-looking man, swarthy, somewhat grizzled, handsome despite a scar coursing upwards on one cheek. He was shorter than nearly all the high school athletes, but his chest seemed to span half an acre. His biceps bulged, accented by his plain gray T-shirt. He was a clean-living man, a model to youth in speech and conduct. "Coach" was strong, gentle but firm, understanding, loyal and quiet, and patient in teaching. He wanted to win, but only in fair combat. He played by the rules.

Responding to pressure from one of my best friends, I reported for track tryouts during the spring of 1937. For some inexplicable reason, I decided to focus on running distances, principally the mile run. Glen Cunningham had recently impressed the world with his record. I decided to throw in my lot with Cunningham, who had overcome childhood polio to become a champion.

The first afternoon of practice that spring, Scheidt sent his veteran athletes to the infield and track to begin their procedures. He divided the new aspirants into two groups, one to appear in running events, and the other in field. I waited with the new runners—spindly, not too promising adolescents—who sat expectantly in a huddle or stretched out on a grassy slope. Scheidt walked up to us and said succinctly: "Fellows, I have only three rules for runners: Get started, keep going and finish well. Now, let's go."

I was mildly stunned. I thought Coach would provide some magical formula that would turn us from stumbling, lazy dolts into lithe, swift runners. As it turned out, however, that was the last time I even thought about putting down this man in any way. He coached winners.

Scheidt's simple formula, repeated to us from time to time, ultimately became an important influence in my life. As time went on, I recognized the parallels between his six-word principle and Christian truth. It fit biblical analogy well. On numerous occasions I have passed along the same words to others when they needed counsel in personal problem-solving.

Perhaps I have attributed more to Scheidt's pattern than he meant by it, but are not wise sayings of good men and women expandable to larger meaning than even they would at first anticipate? What I learned from that track coach expanded to life concepts: *Get Started, Keep Going, Finish Well*. They still belong to me as effective motivational factors nearly 60 years after I first heard them.

Get Started

"Get Started" was the first of the three pairs of Scheidt's words. Expressed as a command, these words also imply a sense of motivation. Proper motivation means not only having right reasons for what we do, but also right feelings.

We must desire to do what we are supposed to do if we are to do it at all, and if we are to do it well.

It is common to desire to "do something important," to achieve above the ordinary. Parents look for a glimmer of this ambition in their children, no matter how faint, and if they detect none, they may try to stir some up.

Similarly, teachers try to stimulate their students to desire to learn and to accomplish. Often their efforts are met with apathy. Students devote much energy and creativity to constructing barriers to keep themselves from the experiences and involvements that would launch them into effective living. Teachers can find ways to go over, under or around these barriers.

Anyone who works with teenagers knows how hard some of them work to avoid growing up. They seem to hide in the "stuff" of their pop culture. Although deferring the hard issues that bring growth may seem easier to them at the time, the high road to maturity is the road that will bring long-term happiness. Adults give too little attention to helping youths overcome this common resistance to development.

Self-motivation is one of the issues of development that wise parents and teachers must aim to inspire in youth. Youth need an inner desire to learn, labor and achieve on their own. External motivations like power, money and recognition are not enough. Such rewards are attractive and honorable, if honorably engaged, but they need perspective.

For maturing men and women, personal motivations are more meaningful than the more common, measurable rewards of an affluent society. Without satisfactory fulfillment of inner spiritual motivations like understanding, wisdom, creativity, love, service and devotion, they are not likely to be fulfilled with external rewards.

A key to inner motivation is inspiration. Knute Rockne knew this. Rockne, the eminent football coach at Notre Dame early in the 20th century, could take an ordinary team and turn it into a winning one simply by adding inspiration to excellent instruction in the fundamentals of football. Rockne is known for his "Win one for the Gipper" story.

George Gipp was a gifted football player. Had he lived, Gipp might have become a lasting star in the sports firmament, but Gipp died prematurely. It is reported that on his deathbed he told Rockne that one day the coach would need another inspirational tactic to turn a defeat toward victory. "Win one for the Gipper," he said.

The story goes that Rockne held the idea until one Saturday after Gipp's death. He used Gipp's deathbed suggestion and literally turned his team from defeat to victory that day. Jack Chevigny, a star player, made the winning touchdown, and while standing in the end zone in tears, called aloud to the air: "Gipp, we did it! We did it for you!"

Rockne's stories illustrate the vitality of inspiration fused to motivation. Another Rockne tale involves an alleged event focusing on the life of Rockne's six-year-old son. The Notre Dame team was weak that year. Notre Dame was scheduled to play a strong Georgia Tech team, and sports writers were predicting a Georgia rout. The travel schedule was tight, but the train for Atlanta was delayed in South Bend because Rockne was late. When he arrived at last, he rushed to his seat and sank down in a funk. He sat silent, solemn in spirit. He did not chat amiably with his players or fellow coaches, which was unusual for Rockne.

When they arrived and the game began, Rockne seemed almost uninterested. Assistant coaches appeared to take over. The game's first half was dismal for Notre Dame, fulfilling predictions. It appeared that Notre Dame would lose by a high score and would be humiliated. In the locker room at half time, Rockne began his remarks by reading aloud several telegrams from prominent football players. But then he abruptly stopped reading and folded the papers in his hands.

According to the story, a solemn Rockne apologized for his attitude and conduct on the trip. He explained the cause for his distress. He said that his son, almost a team mascot and well-known to the players, had suddenly contracted a mysterious illness just as Rockne was leaving home to catch the Georgia-bound train. Rockne reported taking the boy to the hospital, waiting there as long as he felt he could for word from the physician. He said he had finally left the lad and his mother there and hurried to the train. Rockne explained that he would have been informed if there had been any change in the boy's condition, but that he had received no word from home.

After finishing his story, Rockne again apologized to the team for his dilatory coaching and inadequate attention to the players. He told them that his son, even in the midst of his illness, had sent his childish words of greeting and his hopes for winning. As Rockne concluded his remarks in solemn tone and mien, a period of silence fell upon the men. Some players, hunched over in front of the lockers, wept.

When they hit the field a short time later, the Notre Dame team played the second half of the game like men who could not lose. Georgia Tech gained a few yards, whereas Notre Dame scored several times and won the game. The turnaround of the second half was nearly unbelievable.

Exhausted but happy, the players sauntered, with much backslapping, toward the locker room. They were interrupted by a six-year-old lad racing toward them, yelling, "My daddy's team won! My daddy's team won!"

A perspiring and surprised tackle lifted the boy in his arms. The boy responded with nothing short of ecstasy.

"But you are supposed to be in the hospital in South Bend," the player said. "What happened?"

"My dad told Mother to bring me on another train and not let you fellas see us 'til after the game," the boy explained. Then he repeated excitedly, "You won—my daddy's team won!"

Little wonder the world of sports remembers Rockne as a great motivator. Who would believe games of such magnitude could be won on a coach's ruse? Certainly inspiration like Rockne provided can be a key to motivation.

For the Christian, motivation does not depend on inspiring fabrications. The stakes are infinitely higher than winning a football game. Motivation for the Christian is found in the truth of God manifested in the Person of Jesus Christ. When we stumble along and sometimes fall, it is because we do not believe in Him strongly enough to compete well in the life game.

It is important to make a strong start in the Christian life—and in any activity worth doing. My first start in the mile run for West High School in my hometown proved a humbling illustration of this truth. I had practiced for that race as I had been coached, and I prayed to win. In fact I had never prayed so sincerely.

At the starting line that afternoon I set the chocks, crouched, lifted, and at the crack of the gun was away. An instant later the pistol sounded twice, informing us that someone had made a false start leaving the blocks too soon. I was the guilty party.

Returning to the starting line, I determined not to err again. When the next start was made, I was last to leave the line. I followed the pack.

It took me several weeks to discover the perfect timing that would make starts legal and effective. Poor starts can often lose races. They are disheartening. They put one to disadvantage which may be impossible to overcome in the remainder of the race.

False starts seriously threaten persons and even societies. This is dramatically illustrated in the wilderness experience of Israel told in Numbers 14. Moses, preparing to enter the Promised Land, sent spies to determine the circumstances of the invasion. The spies' majority report did not favor entrance, however, and the army of Israel concurred. So Israel made preparations for nomadic life in the wilderness. Although disappointed over the lost opportunity, Moses would make the best of it.

When the people perceived their mistake, however, they

reversed themselves and determined, against Moses' counsel, to invade the land. Moses knew they would fail. He knew that the moment had been lost.

But the army rejected Moses' counsel and mobilized to attack the Canaanites. Moses refused to lead them. After the Israelites were soundly defeated, they retreated to the wilderness and to Moses. For the following nearly 40 years they wandered until another generation emerged to win the land. Throughout the wilderness trek, Israel is represented as lacking in maturity, a lack that cost them a great deal.

An opportunity may only present itself once. The ancient Romans realized this, and are remembered for shouting, *"Carpe diem"*—"Seize the day." Conversely, Pharaoh is remembered as a man who "missed his opportunity" (Jeremiah 46:17).

There is evidence to show how remarkable the life of someone who starts well can be. Persons who are most fully gratified in their later years usually started with worthwhile motivations that they acted upon at appropriate times. Youths who are motivated to make life decisions early and to follow through to action, have advantage. They seek educations, set purposes and follow productive experiences that will affirm their spiritual, social, intellectual and physical lives. But even lacking an ideal start, one may find a way to begin when he understands the principle: Get Started.

Keep Going

Scheidt's second pair of words was: "Keep going." To "never give up" was Coach Scheidt's belief. He respected the fellows who cultivated their own reasons for competing. They did what had to be done because they wanted to, not just because physical education classes were compulsory. Nevertheless, perseverance was so important to Coach that he would force the issue even with the men who possessed less than ideal inner motivation. Perseverance is more important than is generally recognized. The concept of perseverance is major in the Scriptures, and shows itself a factor in everyday life.

Coach would walk or jog along the track, shouting at runners with some gusto: "Keep going! Keep going! Come on now, keep going!" I would finish my laps. I would keep going. Although I did not understand why I should keep going, something inside me said this was good for me to do. But usually I did not want to do it—and usually I did not win races.

On one occasion we were scheduled to run at the city track meet where several high schools would be participating. The number of students in the mile run was large, so we crowded to the starting line with the designated best runners up front. I was somewhere back in the pack. Runners could earn points by being among the first 15 finishers—the first runner to cross the line earned 15 points and the 15th earned one. By the time 15 men had crossed the finish line nearly five minutes later, I had completed little more than three of four laps.

Recognizing that there were no more points to earn, I loped off the track onto the infield. Almost immediately Coach Scheidt headed for me, walking past fellows who had completed the race and earned points. He faced me, lifting his hand to my shoulder. In a firm but even voice he said, "Mark, if you ever do that again—stop in a race just because you can't win points—you will not run for West High as long as I am coach."

I protested feebly that the meet was over, that the people were leaving for home, and that one more lap didn't make any difference. He responded with a statement I have never forgotten: "The crowd will be coming down out of the stands; the sun will be setting in the west; you push your way through to the finish. We will hold the bus for you." And he walked away. I will never forget Scheidt's perceptive admonition.

This is not to say, however, that one should never quit. Not all projects begun are worth concluding. Circumstances change, even values change. There are teams that I wish to quit, and should. Either they, or I, have changed course. I do not expect to have only my way, so I withdraw to permit others to accomplish their purposes. But there ought to be dignity in terminating participation. One must have his own good reasons to stay or to resign—reasons, not excuses. But when we are on the right team, we need to persevere.

A key to perseverance is the achievement of a second wind gained when runners maintain themselves faithfully in their assignments. We were taught that if we conditioned ourselves and used our bodies according to their conditioning, we might expect to experience a euphoric "second wind."

Applying Coach Scheidt's words to my running, I eventually understood firsthand the miracle of the second wind. I ran those seemingly interminable laps with legs heavy, arms in the way and lungs screaming for air. All of a sudden one day, something happened that changed everything. The rhythm, the pace, the feeling, all seemed to belong to someone else. I was a different runner, doing a marvelous thing. I felt as if I could run all day.

It appears that nearly every life activity requires a kind of second wind. Often happily married couples perceive themselves to be twice-married to the same spouse: once, on the day of the wedding, and again, years later, when they determine to maintain their marriage. Most divorces are the result of failing to follow through to a second and sustaining experience, one born of commitment rather than emotion.

Fern Erway and I were married on September 18, 1943. We lived for some years with less than a totally satisfactory relationship. We would not divorce, but our marriage was often under tension. Recognizing our disappointment, we made a new and dramatic affirmation of our marriage one Saturday in April 1957. We decided that we would achieve what we believed our marriage ought to be. From that date on, our second decision made marriage for us something magnificent and fulfilling.

Similarly, successful collegians may enter formal higher education twice: once when they enroll, and then again when they determine to remain in school. If they graduate, it is because they have made both decisions—to begin, and later, to keep going. The second decision, verifying the first, overcomes homesickness, romantic distractions, economic uncertainty, uneven academic performance, and other problems, to complete degree requirements. About half of entering freshmen do not graduate. Most of these did not reaffirm their first goal of college entrance.

The Christian experience follows similar patterns. We approach the cross and the empty tomb following our initial call to repentance and salvation. Although aware of the ultimate benefit of commitment to Jesus Christ, we find our lives do not demonstrate the changes we had believed would occur. Should we resign from the Christian congregation and return to the life from which we came? Some persons do. Others, rather than drop out, turn to the risen Christ and the Holy Spirit, seeking additional resources. They keep returning for fresh sustenance. This is part of Christian sanctification and the highway to spiritual maturity.

Our efforts to live the Christian life often weary us. By confessing that weariness and claiming the available spiritual resources, we gain a second wind. The Person of the Holy Spirit strengthens us with larger provision than we formerly knew. We gain special resources to achieve appropriate spiritual and human goals. By that miracle we get on, not alone, but in the sanctification of Christ through the Holy Spirit. At this point we discover the difference between ordinary Christian life and mature Christian life. We then enjoy what some Bible teachers have called "the abundant life."

Finish Well

Coach's third pair of words was: "Finish well." For me the principle relates to sustaining to the end what has already been well-begun. American poet Robert Frost reminded us in one of his oft-quoted verses that the last is the reason the first was made. It is a truth commonly missed. To finish life in the manner I ought indicates maturity and results in triumph. For me, my marriage, my professional and educational goals, my spiritual growth—these have been and continue to be important matters to which I give my continuous attention. I cannot coast—each day contributes another piece to the finished work.

Triumph in the sense we use it here does not mean being first among others, but being first with oneself. In creating my own competition, I also keep my own score. Triumph does not mean that one person is better than all the others, but rather that he or she is performing at his or her own best. When I decided to create my own self-competition, I became a significantly better performer. In the matter of marriage, although I was doing better than most married men I counseled, I saw that my own performance was inadequate. I realized I could not use troubled men as my models—I had to seek my own potential, my own first place that I was capable of achieving.

In nearly everything I do, it is possible for me to perform at a first, second, third, fourth or even lower level. When I decided to be a first-rate husband rather than a second-rate one, my marriage flourished as it had not before. But even when I was functioning as a second-rate husband, I was not functioning as poorly as I could have. Although my marriage seemed to flounder, it could have been worse. I could have declined further to my third or fourth levels. The possibilities downward will always remain, and on occasion, I have slipped into some of them. On such occasions, I am revulsed at my conduct and attitudes. Of course the principle applies in other avenues of life as well. I was sometimes a better teacher or administrator than I was on other occasions. But when I was less than I could have been, I lost.

During his last weeks of life, Jim Valvano recognized this concept of winning. Valvano, a 47-year-old former basketball coach for North Carolina State and successful sports commentator on national television, won the attention of sports enthusiasts during 1992 and 1993 when he learned he was dying of cancer. As Valvano reflected on his life, he told the story of an encounter he had with players when he, at 23 years of age, began coaching at a small college. "Why is winning so important to you?" the students asked Valvano.

"Because the final score defines you," he said. "You lose, ergo, you're a loser. You win, ergo, you're a winner."

But the students argued that participation was the reason for playing. They said that for them the main thing was discovering how to be their own best—whether the score favored them or not. It took more than two decades, along with intense suffering in his fight with cancer, however, until Valvano was willing to say, "Those kids were right. It's effort, not result. It's trying. . . . What a great human being I could have been if I'd had this awareness back then." [3]

Perhaps it was Paul's understanding of these principles that caused him to choose footracing as a good way to illustrate the type of sportsmanship necessary for winning life's spiritual contest. Racing, unlike today's football, is not a collision of bodies. It is a sport that provides freedom for people to do their own best, knowing that champions before them beckon them forward to greater achievement. They set a pace and a record, and then they invited them to similar or better achievement. They would not be offended at any improvements over their own performances. Old champions tend to admire new ones. They were winners, and others can be winners, too: "Records are made to be broken."

When we study serious competitors in the race of life, we learn that these people have in common several fundamental perceptions:

1. *They practice life seriously in order to be counted worthy to play the game.* They willingly carry responsibility. They do not wait for life's meaning to come to them; they seek it. They are not in the stands but on the playing field.

"Spectatoritis" generates frustration in today's society. Created to participate, people may nevertheless be reluctant to join the field because they are not aware of their own potential. Studies have been made to discover why audiences at sporting events seem to be aggressive, so aggressive that persons are sometimes injured or killed by other spectators. Researchers conclude that onlookers apparently would like to enter the game, but their places in the bleachers do not allow for that, so they invoke their aggression in illegitimate ways.

2. *After being counted worthy to play, serious competitors play the game to win.* They expect results, and are willing to take risks, feeling some pain and weariness in order to achieve results. They are dedicated, giving their time and energy. They understand that winning requires effort, practice, self-denial, patience and adherence to guidelines. They are not driven by the need for immediate gratification like those who use drugs for a quick fix. Competitors are willing to patiently and consistently exert the effort to get the results.

3. *They give all they ought to give.* They perform by aiming to achieve their own first place. They believe in what they are doing. They play out their own roles and not those of others. These serious competitors learn that they need to do the right things, in the right way and at the right time. All three "rights" need to be present. Godly winning implies this kind of commitment.

As we apply these fundamentals to our lives we will begin to experience personal triumph. And as we experience triumph, we will see our faith increase—not only our faith in God, but also our faith in our own potential to become mature in thoughts, attitudes and in life itself. This kind of faith depends on the biblical concepts of patience and endurance; believers are commanded to endure in their faith, to endure to the end (see Luke 21:19).

Even though we are not in life competition with others, by applying these principles we will likely outlast most of the others anyway. Many competitors give up too soon. Survivors believe there is more to be gained at the end of the line than dropouts believe can be found. Dropouts will not stay in—they will not finish and reap the benefits that would have accrued. They lose, not because they were beaten by the competition, but because they drop out.

Peter Gillquist, writing for *Christianity Today*, suggests that part of the cause for this attrition may have to do with a changed emphasis among Christians in the Church:

> There is a curious difference between modern and ancient views of the Christian life. Today we emphasize the New Birth; the ancients emphasized being faithful to the end. We moderns talk of wholeness and purposeful living; they spoke of the glories of the eternal kingdom.
>
> This is not to say the early saints ignored initial conversion, nor does it mean we today have forgotten about the eternal kingdom. But the emphasis in our attention has been shifted from the completing of the Christian life to the beginning of it.[4]

Gillquist further states that contemporary Christians are our heroes, those in the current limelight. For the ancients, the heroes were those who had already finished the course (see Hebrews 11-12:2). For us, current celebrities have replaced genuine heroes. Celebrities are seldom heroes.

The concept of finishing well projects to the future. Whether we run a race or guide a plow or ride a rocket, the destination is everything, and the immediate situation is relatively unimportant except as it affects worthy objectives. This perception of endings is contrary to the popular view held by those who are not so much concerned with destiny as they are with the journey. They may not know where they are going, but they are on their way.

The apostle Paul viewed his life, from his conversion forward, as preparation for the key moment—the moment when he would cross the finish line. From the point of conversion on, he moved continuously toward an upward goal. This perception of the apostle's purpose and belief is helpful in interpreting and applying his writings. We learn to act in ways that assure spiritual growth through to the close of life. However, if the believer, like the undisciplined runner, looks too much to others, or if he looks backward to former things, or even downward at his feet, he will likely break pace or stumble. He should instead focus on ending well. At the finish line, maturity becomes perfection.

In the 1954 Empire Games, Englishman Roger Bannister illustrated to the world the benefit of keeping one's eyes fixed on the finish line. Bannister, who earlier in the year had been the first person to run the mile in under four minutes, was bested in time by John Landy. The two met in Vancouver, B.C., to discover who was supreme.

John Landy led the race almost all the way. He made the last turn and the goal was in sight. But at this critical point, for some reason which even he could not explain later, Landy thrust his chin over his shoulder to see where Bannister was. In doing so, Landy slightly broke his stride and rhythm and Bannister was able to pass him and win the race.

A photograph of Landy's look-back won a prize for the most unusual published snapshot in sports that year. When asked what he was looking for, peering over his shoulder, Landy replied, "I was looking for a stone to hide under."[5]

It is easy to look back at other participants. We complain to God, "Lord, what about him?" But God answers, "What is that to you? You must follow me" (John 21:21-22). The race is in ourselves as individuals and the pacesetter is Christ.

In times past, some track runners depended on pacesetters to motivate them. Each quarter mile, a pacesetter, fresh for that segment of the race, would enter the track and set a standard for the other runners who were growing fatigued. Eventually this practice was no longer permitted, and runners had to do something else for motivation.

Gil Dodds had depended on pacesetters. Dodds was an unlikely candidate to break the world record for the mile. He was short, stocky, thick-thighed and bespectacled—not the typical image of a runner. But Dodds' coach knew how to motivate him, and Dodds willingly submitted to his instruction. At first Dodds ran against local city competition until he could win in every meet, then he ran against all New England competition, and then against champions along the Atlantic seaboard. At last Dodds entered national meets. He began each new level as a loser, but encouraged by his coach, Dodds remained on the circuit to win. He was, by the mid-1940s, virtually unbeatable in the United States.

Still, Dodds was intimidated at the thought of breaking a record for the mile. I knew Dodds when he announced that he would retire from competition. But once more, his coach managed to inspire him with a fresh challenge for the record. Dodds protested that he could not achieve a record because he could not run well enough without a fast man setting pace for him. He knew he could outrun competition, but he did not have the confidence that he could do so well without someone to set the pace on the track. Dodds himself in 1945 had become the standard to be matched or surpassed, even by Dodds.

But Dodds' coach had an answer: "I have a standard you will go by." The coach pulled out his stopwatch and said, "This." The coach calculated a time that Dodds would have to beat to set the new record, and then told him to let the stopwatch be his pacesetter.

And he did. He won, setting a record, because he was the best "Dodds" he could be that night, and Chicago Stadium could barely contain the crowd's exuberant celebration. I was there and saw what a champion can accomplish.

Fortunately for us, we do not need to set pace with some device for motivation. We have the ultimate pacesetter, Jesus Christ. We will never surpass our model, but we will become the best we can become if we follow His pace. Our duty is to know and to follow the course of life to our highest pinnacle of achievement. That highest point is full maturity. If I do achieve maturity, I will finish well. Now that I am in the latter period of my life, spiritual maturity is nearly all that I want from my remaining years. To finish well will affect virtually everything of value to me for life and immortality.

With the records set by the saints of the past, serious Christians will be encouraged that they too can win. But the race for each of us is our own. No matter what the external competition, when I have given my best, I win. I win against all the lesser, weaker persons I might have been.

"I have fought the good fight, I have finished the race, I have kept the faith" (2 Timothy 4:7).

Endnotes

1 Hendrick, Bill. "Stress Playing Havoc with Baby Boomers," *Minneapolis Star-Tribune*, July 4, 1993, pp. 1-5.

2 Balog, Kathy. "Scoring in Business," *USA Today*, May 18, 1995, p. B-1. Copyright 1995, USA Today. Reprinted with permission.

3 Smith, Gary. "Tough Lesson," *Reader's Digest*, June 1993, pp. 11-12. (summarizing Gary Smith in *Sports Illustrated*.)

4 Gillquist, Peter. "A Marathon We Mean to Win," *Christianity Today*, October 23, 1981, p. 22.

5 Rosenbaum, Art. "Fainting at the Finish," *San Francisco Chronicle*, May 7, 1979, p. 52.

Chapter 2

Finishing Well

And here is my advice about what is best for you in this matter: Last year you were the first not only to give but also to have the desire to do so. Now finish the work, so that your eager willingness to do it may be matched by your completion of it, according to your means. For if the willingness is there, the gift is acceptable according to what one has, not according to what he does not have. (2 Corinthians 8:10-12)

The continuing physical need of Christians in cities outside of Corinth was likely the occasion for this section of the apostle's letter. There was apparently a serious problem, perhaps a general famine in Judea and Jerusalem, which the Corinthian believers had responded to with a relief project a year earlier than this writing. Although they were eager at the beginning, now their interest flagged. Paul wrote to urge them to continue with the much-needed support.

In his letter, the apostle enlarged on a basic pattern of conduct that he had hoped would be evident among the Corinthian believers. The desirable pattern is to begin appropriate projects with right attitudes and maintain those projects through to the end with right attitudes. The Corinthians began relief work, a work they very much desired to do. But a year later interest may have declined and effort lessened. The apostle was concerned that their loss of interest might end their participation.

Paul reminded them to maintain the work, but also to maintain their zeal. The apostle was convinced that a project launched in God's will with appropriate zeal was to be completed with that same genuine fervency. At the beginning of the project, highly focused holy animation produced excitement in the Corinthian church. But as the project continued, the Corinthians may have attached higher status to giving generous amounts of relief than to the spirit of giving. Feeling they had done their part, the members might have decided to leave unfinished tasks to others who seemed to have done less than they ought to have done. The apostle, then, wrote about two matters: 1) that the Corinthians continue their project of giving and 2) that they continue in the spirit with which they had begun.

Paul reminded the Corinthians that nothing was requested of them beyond their competency to perform, with zealous attitudes. Zeal leads to mature decision-making about serving. It is an antidote to prevailing cynical and amoral attitudes in society. Holy excitement in life and ministry is a sign of sensitive faith in God.

Like the Corinthians at the time of Paul's second letter, our generation also may not regard God's work with sufficient holy excitement. Even if we do not fail God in action, we often fail Him in attitude. We may give generously to God's work, but not catch the Bible's teaching about stewardship. We should not give, grousing all the while, "Why doesn't somebody else give now? We gave last year, why should we do it again?" Scripture teaches that we should never cease in giving where needed, and that Christians should give with an animated spirit. The Lord loves a "hilarious" giver. By implication, one should not bother to give at all, if he or she is giving reluctantly. Christians must feel the joy of ministry if that ministry is to have virtue in it.

Failed attitudes often lead to failed actions. The principle of joyful tenacity is, or ought to be, larger than any problem to be solved. It is a way of life. Vibrant men and women sustain joyful service with joyful attitudes. Attitude is an important initial consideration for reaching maturity.

A modern example helps us relate to the issues of the famine in Jerusalem. During the mid-1980s, the media, principally television, informed the world of widespread famine in central and western Africa. Watching nightly television news programs showing the distended-bellied children and the emotionless, skeleton-like adults, all dying of starvation, the giving public poured out foodstuffs and medical supplies in a flood. Many tons of food were flown to the troubled sites. Supporting agencies airlifted trucks to move food cartons into the hinterlands. Donor nations sometimes paid import duty to get by intransigent government agencies in order to feed dying men, women and children. From San Francisco, where I lived, leading television newscasters collected large donations and personally took medicines and food by chartered planes to Africa. Their poignant stories became leads on news programs for days.

As the weeks went by, however, the stories faded and eventually disappeared. The media no longer reported about the famine, and the matter was largely forgotten in the public mind. Did the news coverage cease because there was recovery? It might surprise people to learn that although famine did abate in some areas, it continued and even worsened in others. Moreover, a few years later other nations like India were numbered with the suffering in Africa as famine spread to their part of the globe.

The project was not finished, but many persons were finished with it. Although much was done, the problem nevertheless escalated. And because relief did not continue until the problem was solved, the massive early effort merely delayed the starvation of millions. During 1992, stimulated by new catastrophes including the Russian national collapse, agencies tried to revive the public interest of the mid-1980s. They had only mixed response.

Many persons and institutions finish poorly. They seem to be marching downhill to concentration camps in dismal spirit. They often begin well, but crumple later. Arnold Toynbee, the eminent British historian, noted that every civilization eventually comes to an end. In his historical theorizing, Toynbee used a model that showed roads winding their way around and upward on a mountain. The roads represented various major civilizations, but each of the roads came to a dead end. He felt that civilizations should not have to die. But they do.

The point for us is that great historical civilizations did not finish well. They followed a common path to oblivion. That repetitive dead-end pattern stands to warn living nations. And it ought to warn each individual about his or her own end.

The tendency for all things to decay is sufficiently strong that we tend to factor it in. Decay is projected even when all is well and improving. The University of Washington has written over its facade: "The University of a Thousand Years." Why only a thousand? Why will it die? Even Adolf Hitler during the mid-1930s limited his expectations for the Nazi Third Reich when he announced it was set "for a thousand years." It lasted little more than a decade.

Dead ends are not inevitable. We can build our lives in succeeding elevations, where each successive step moves forward. Horace Greeley stated this concept well in a memorial to Abraham Lincoln. Although he was no admirer of Lincoln during the President's administration, Greeley later gave Lincoln one of the greatest compliments ever afforded by a man to a man: "There was probably no year of his life when he was not a wiser, cooler and better man than he had been the year preceding."

This ought to apply to Christians as they invest their

years in God's service. It should be said of each Christian
that there was no year of life when he or she was a wiser,
cooler and better Christian than during the current one.
But to become more mature—more Christlike—with each
passing year, we need to familiarize ourselves with barriers
that prevent us from finishing well.

We May Not Finish Well Because of Human Frailty

The biblical account contains many references to spiritual decline caused by the human condition. Knowledgeable Bible students could make their own lists of these
accounts. They make worthy Bible study.

During a leadership forum, Joe Aldrich, college president, made an important observation about individuals
who finish poorly. He said, "It's scary to realize that most
of the people who failed in Scripture failed in the second
half of their lives. Moses, Solomon, Hezekiah, Saul, and
others failed as older men." Aldrich added: "I am in the
most dangerous period of my life right now."[1]

Examining the lives of the men Aldrich mentioned, as
well as other men in Scripture, we find patterns emerging.
Men who failed to finish well fell into one or more catego-
ries—they became weary, or proud, or fell to some other
human weakness. They may have even forgotten the one
true God, preferring to remake Him according to their own
ideas.

After decades of faithfulness, Noah was found drunk,
perhaps falling down drunk, in his tent. He seems to have
let down his guard after many years of working and waiting. Noah may have wished "to get away from it all." He
who successfully built history's most famous ship, preaching as he worked, subsequently riding out the most extensive of all floods, ends, in our narrative about him, drunk
and cursing his family (see Genesis 9:20-27).

We cannot say that Noah finished well, certainly not as

well as he might have. As the story is given to us, the last of
his life was marked negatively by his drunkenness and
grossness. This lapse does not mean that Noah lost his
faith or became a bad man. It means that he did not complete his course in the manner in which he should have
completed it. What a man of spiritual distinction Noah was
before and during the flood. But perhaps the year of isolation on the ark took its toll. One could wish that the biblical story of Noah had ended with the opening of the hatch
on the ark after the flood waters subsided.

Later, Moses made a less than ideal finish when he,
through sin, lost his privilege of entering the Promised
Land. He was angry, and that anger caused him to act im-
maturely. During the wilderness trek, Moses was deeply
angry from time to time. Anger seems to have been his be-
setting sin. He found water for thirsty Israel in one strike
upon a rock on the trek at Horeb (see Exodus 17:6). On the
occasion at Meribah, however, he was told to merely speak
to the rock. Instead he struck, not once, but twice (see
Numbers 20:8-13). In his anger at the complaints of the
people, Moses reacted fiercely, disregarding divine instruc-
tions. That presumption later cost him the privilege of entering Canaan beyond Jordan.

Most readers reviewing Moses' 40 years of wilderness
leadership would say that he performed well and with remarkable success. Artists and sculptors have been intrigued
with the figure of Moses, larger than life, leading a sometimes recalcitrant people to home and safety. To have led a
million people through four decades of wilderness trek-
king, a nation without visible means of support, was certainly high achievement. After years of learning obedience
through dramatic lessons, Moses should have been obedient at Meribah as he saw the end of the four decades' journey. For Moses, it must have been crushing failure to
forfeit the hoped-for goal of standing on promised land.
But many years of faithful service by aging prophets does
not give them the privilege to disobey.

Elijah, following the Mount Carmel showdown between God and the prophets of Baal, fled from the scene of victory, stopping at last to rest and fret under a juniper tree. There he complained about his plight, preferring his own death as a way out of personal stress. Perhaps bodily and emotionally weary from the Carmel triumph, Elijah was taken with a common mental-emotional illness, the "poor me's."

Elijah's flight and complaint became cause for the beginning of the end of his ministry and its transfer to Elisha. At the tree he was instructed to anoint Elisha in his room (1 Kings 19:16). This all points to the conclusion that Elijah did not finish ministry as well as he should have finished. Elijah's exit in the fiery chariot, implying approval of the prophet, does not change that evaluation. Like Noah and others of high achievement we might name, Elijah did not lose immortality. But there could have been even more for them at the end of their courses.

This pattern of decline is well illustrated in the experience of King Asa. Youthful Asa was elevated to the throne of Judah. In Second Chronicles 14:2, we read: "Asa did what was good and right in the eyes of the LORD his God." The biblical record follows, in some detail, the decades of Asa's accomplishments. It is said that Asa removed foreign altars, high places and sacred pillars and cut down the Asherim (wooden images of female deities), and so restored to the nation faith in Jehovah, a faith based on the Scriptures. The Bible records that Asa brought peace to the nation, primarily through trust in God and the development of defensive rather than offensive military preparations. Finally, Asa became prosperous, partly through the plunder of the invading armies that attacked Judah and lost, and partly through effective public planning.

Asa's full commitment and effective program for the good of his people brought revival to Judah. Citizens from the northern kingdom of Israel began defecting to the southern kingdom to join the society of the Lord, and of Asa. Asa played no favorites, supporting righteous equity to the point of removing the status of his mother as Queen Mother because she set up a pagan idol. For decades Judah was at peace. It was a highly commendable period in Judah's history. Few nations have been better managed than Judah was under Asa.

After reigning for 35 years, however, Asa was confronted with an ancient version of the Berlin Wall erected by Baasha, king of Israel, to prevent citizens from defecting southward, and perhaps also to prevent Judeans from traveling northward into Israel. The act unsettled Asa. Turning from defensive to aggressive military procedures, Asa made a treaty purchasing mercenary soldiers from Ben Hadad, king in Damascus. Asa used treasures from the kingdom and the temple to pay the bill. This use of God's resources for the purpose of military aggression was a major blunder. From Damascus, Ben Hadad launched attacks on Baasha; Asa's Judean forces attacked from the south, ending in the defeat of Israel.

But Hanani, the prophet, rebuked Asa for buying pagan support rather than trusting God, who had given victories in Asa's early reign and had provided lasting peace following those first "shakedown" years. That early trying period and the ensuing years of divine blessing so well administered by Asa created context for Hanani to affirm a spiritual truth: "For the eyes of the LORD range throughout the earth to strengthen those whose hearts are fully committed to him" (2 Chronicles 16:9). Asa, in his earlier reign, was the human inspiration for the statement. With the introduction of aggressive military action, however, God promised Asa, through the prophet Hanani, that Judah would from then on continue to be at war. The blessed decades of peace were ended. Asa's bright and lengthy reign had tarnished.

But Asa's deterioration did not end there. Other conduct uncharacteristic of Asa occurred during the final six years of his reign. Angry at the critical prophet, Asa jailed Hanani. The king also introduced limited oppression, perhaps oppressing the citizens who supported Hanani.

Within four years after initiating war against Baasha, Asa contracted a disease in his feet. Relying upon physicians to help him, he forgot to seek the Lord (see 2 Chronicles 16:12). Earlier his reliance would have been on God, and only after prayer would he turn to physicians. But Asa's drift was not merely a temporary lapse—the new negative pattern was set. Two years later Asa was dead.

Asa, a king serving with dynamic spiritual faith for the first 85 percent of his reign, did not finish well. Cut the last six years out of Asa's 41-year reign, and we possess the story of a nearly perfect state and monarch. Was it a kind of weariness in well-doing that overcame the king? Was there an erosion of Asa's sense of glory and awe related to God?

Frailty enters not only the bones and muscles, but the spirit, leading to anger, boredom, self-pity or other manifestations. Spiritual, emotional and even social weariness may have become the uninvited companions to Asa in his later life.

Aging, with its accompaniments, steals away perceptions of reality, fooling us into a belief that we are exempt from standard considerations and duty. We have noted that growing old is not synonymous with maturity. Many elderly persons are crotchety, which is like behavior observed in a spoiled child. But aging ought to be a time of fulfillment for the person of God with special endurance for faith and life. Scripture teaches about wisdom and the hoary head. Most societies rightly expect virtue and wisdom from their elders. It is a period for patience and prayer, for courage and spiritual maturity, and for modeling.

Our experiences may be similar to those of others who did not finish well because of frailty in the human spirit and body. Our attitudes and spirits decline faster than our bodies decline. We appear unwilling to motivate ourselves to continuing freshness, creativity, and virtue. When we grow weary of our way, and do nothing about our attitudes, we are almost assured that we will not finish well, or well enough.

A marriage commonly fails because of the ravages of human frailty in one or both spouses. A husband or wife becomes weary of hearing the same voice, doing the same things, eating the same menus. Men and women are generally too lazy or dull of mind to introduce creativity into everyday life. So much seems "old." Inadvertently, boredom overtakes us and hangs on.

Boredom leads to folly. An individual may even weary of intimacy with the same spouse in marriage, and may look elsewhere for a new companion, a new scintillation. It is clear that boredom is dangerous, and variety becomes a value to be sought. We forget, as Asa must have forgotten in his last years, that God can revive lives and maintain them. We also forget, if we ever knew, that to maintain our lives as they ought to be maintained, they must be renewed in their parts from time to time.

The point is readily illustrated from common experiences. Church members lose their way, becoming weary in well-doing. Eventually bored and without conviction, some tend to do the same churchy things, just as they may tend to go through repeated motions in all else. They begin skipping duties, skipping God's house and devotions, skipping stewardship, consequently skipping personal and spiritual growth. They hide their omissions in some way, perhaps by distracting attention from their own faults and focusing it on the faults of other persons and institutions. Through such distraction one may temporarily escape giving an account of himself. Maturity, for this person, is elusive.

It is impossible to estimate the number of church members who do not finish well. We may be acquainted with friends who have professed Christ and yet have lost their way. Distancing themselves from the church, they drop out. Even if not physically dropping out of the congregation, they may slip into neutral, doing nothing. They view one church service a week as sufficient for all spiritual duty. Or perhaps even fewer services in the year will suffice. Older men and women may wish to escape duty with the excuse that the young should take on corporate chores and general responsibilities. Such justifications are escapism, cleverly cast. In reality, it is excuse-making, and unacceptable.

Young people, however, are no more immune to human frailty than the older generation. Collegians often slide into weariness of well-doing in their competitive studies. It is laziness and boredom that reveals itself in various ways, preventing students from finishing well in the college experience—if they finish at all. Often their uncertainties lead to anger and they drop out after fighting their parents, their teachers, their administrators. Of course, some may later turn matters around, and finish well. But at best, this petulance and anger will slow a young person's growth to maturity.

Alumni commonly discuss what they felt and did in college. In 1983, a former student of the college I served at the time, then in San Francisco, attended a friendship banquet where I was the speaker. He had lived his student days 20 years earlier. After the meal, and before dessert was served, he insisted on a private conversation with me. He recited his disappointment of not finishing the college in 1964, of dropping out, of later getting divorced, and of how then, on that night in 1983, he suddenly saw his college days and his life entirely differently.

This former student, now in his middle years, suddenly saw that it was in his hands to complete a project, even complete his life, well. He had turned away from the college, which he had held in low esteem when he dropped out. He had been critical of the faculty of his day, and of just about everyone else he knew related to the institution. But he now understood that these people had cared for students, and he had missed, by his own actions, the benefit of that caring. He said, "For years I have lived just over the hill from here, in south San Francisco, and have never come back. I thought everyone else was out of step. All the time it was I who defeated myself." He was in deep distress.

His story could be repeated by many people with similar experiences, people who may have started well with positive attitudes, but whose attitudes slowly began to decay, even when events did not. When this happens, negative thinking sets in, and not long afterward, negative actions follow. Happily, this decay is avoidable. Many persons do make adjustments in sufficient time to avoid disaster.

A fine fellow, employed at a college where I also worked, wearied of his way. After some tension with the administration, he resigned with an agreement that was mutually acceptable. Some weeks later he asked for reinstatement, not from any fear of unemployment. He was competent, and an attractive candidate for a number of opportunities. He genuinely missed his old assignment. When reminded about his earlier hostility and unhappiness, he replied, "I did not see what I had. I could only accent the negatives. If we decide that negatives prevail, they will." He was caught for a time in negative thinking. Fortunately, he recovered. But when a person persists in negative thinking, it usually means he or she will not finish well.

Whether they finished well or poorly, the people we have discussed so far all made satisfactory beginnings. But good beginnings are not our focus—good endings are. All that begins well does not necessarily end well—as Noah, Asa and the others demonstrate. And to begin poorly does not necessarily preclude finishing well, as the experience of Manasseh, king of Judah, illustrates. But more of him later. Certainly the largest matter is to finish one's whole life, the sum, well.

We May Not Finish Well Because of Pride

The biblical account makes reference to egotism as cause for failure. Three biblical kings—David, Solomon and Nebuchadnezzar—were examples of men who had every necessary provision for finishing well. Nonetheless, their pride interfered with achieving that goal.

David began his public life as a caring and altruistic person, gifted in a variety of ways. Whatever David chose to do he did well—whether it was protecting sheep, playing harps, marshalling soldiers, governing people or writing poetry. He credited God for all that he accomplished.

Later in life he began to credit himself, tacitly at least, for what were the blessings of God. David chose to number the people, perhaps so he could advertise the success of his reign (see 2 Samuel 24). Even his competent but sometimes spiritually insensitive general, Joab, protested the census. But Joab's objection did not deter David, and 70,000 Israelites died when God punished the nation for David's arrogance.

Near the close of David's life, a young virgin, Abishag, was brought to David to lie beside him, providing warmth. Although Scripture states that David was not intimate with his beautiful nurse, we have to wonder if there were not other ways to solve the problem of David's poor blood circulation. Later, tragedy grew out of Abishag's presence in the family, when she became an object of passion for David's son, Adonijah. Adonijah's request for her was a major cause for his execution (1 Kings 2:25). Abishag seems an exploited and tragic figure, and the responsibility for her loss rests heavily on David.

The ancients recognized the principle of starting and finishing well. Long after King David's death, the writer of Chronicles introduced the rise of good King Jehoshaphat to the throne of Judah. He wrote: "And the Lord was with Jehoshaphat because he followed the example of . . . David's earlier days" (2 Chronicles 17:3, NASB). To write about "David's earlier days" may imply something about David's later days. To receive honor for one's youth and silence about one's later life implies decline. David finished less well than he should have. The idiom about "David's earlier days" may have referred to David's precedent reign, with no implication of comparison between first years and later ones. There was, however, a comparison made.

Solomon began his public life with a fully developed state graciously placed in his hands. He could not take credit for early royal accomplishments in the kingdom because all that was necessary had already been done before he assumed the throne. But Solomon seemed unable to manage the prosperity given him, perhaps letting it go to his head. He became indulgent, lavishing time and wealth on buildings, education, pleasures and women. He dabbled extravagantly in this and that, forgetting the source of his inheritance.

Solomon finished so poorly that had God not earlier made the promise that the Son of David, the Messiah, would eventually come from David's kingly line, we are told that the kingdom would have been wrenched from him. David's dynasty would have ended only one generation later with Solomon. Even so, the kingdom was divided upon Solomon's death. The nation split into Israel in the North and Judah in the South (see 1 Kings 11:30-40).

Nebuchadnezzar, king of Babylon, began his public life regally. The Scriptures record a limited period of Nebuchadnezzar's life, but he is well-known from historical and archaeological records. He functioned skillfully to maintain the impressive kingdom his father had bequeathed to him. Like Solomon, he too became extravagant. According to tradition, he constructed one of the wonders of the world, the Hanging Gardens of Babylon. When Nebuchadnezzar took prideful credit for the extensive building and public works, he was not boasting idly—Babylon was impressive. Some of Babylon's ruins remain today, witnessing to the capital achievement of more than 40 years of Nebuchadnezzar's reign.

When we find Nebuchadnezzar in Scripture, he is at a spiritual crossroads. Unfortunately, he chose the dead end of pride and self-honor: "Is this not great Babylon that I have built?" he asked. But the prophet Daniel recorded that God humbled him with temporary insanity leading to a period of isolation in which he lived with the beasts of the field and ate grass like the cattle (Daniel 4:28-33). When he was restored, Nebuchadnezzar wrote that God "is able to humble those who walk in pride" (Daniel 4:37, NASB).

Herod the king, known as Herod the Great in secular history, began public life 40 years before Jesus was born. He may have accomplished as much as any leader in Jerusalem before him. He was a rhetorician, a builder, an administrator, a patron of the arts. Although he had a reputation for cruelty during the decades of his reign, he lost any semblance of balance toward the end. By the time he had served 40 years as a Roman king in Judah, he was a prideful, murderous, spiteful, oily, wizened character, and afraid. Such a person would find it impossible to finish well.

We know enough about the spiritual effects of arrogance on men and nations to realize that egotistical pride is out of place for persons of faith. Humility is necessary for spiritual maturity.

We May Not Finish Well Because of Distortions about God

The biblical account makes reference to humanistic thinking as a cause for not finishing well. Humankind has always been prone to distorting truth—even the ultimate truth of the personhood of God. Gifted people in the Bible—kings, prophets, disciples—were inclined to remake God according to their own ideas. Solomon, whose pride interfered with his finishing well, is an example of someone who distorted the image of God.

Although Solomon was familiar with the Scriptures, he nevertheless suggested an experimental method to ascertain humanity's relationship to God. In Ecclesiastes we read that he experimented seriously, looking for spiritual truth by comparing his human options. While Christians generally have no quarrel with scientific research, we do

object to leaving God out of the equation. And divine revelation did not seem to have been a major part of Solomon's
early experiments. Instead, he tried humanistic directions
like recreation, arts and materialism. Some of Solomon's
experiments resulted in extensive digressions. His wives
and their eclectic religions, for example, turned Solomon
away from the singular God (see 1 Kings 11:4), causing
him to make God into a mosaic of the best pieces from all
religions. But God, as Solomon should have known, is jealous about His exclusive place and nature.

By the time Solomon had concluded that his experiments led to folly, much of his life was already spent. He
had only enough time left to write about his experiences
and to warn others about the vanity of the experimental
route. He emphasized the emptiness of life without God, or
with strange gods.

God's prophet Jonah also created his own distorted image of a god contrary to the God of Scripture. Jonah's was
something of a tribal god. In Jonah's thinking, a tribal god
would always be on the side of the tribe. He would favor
those who use an approved language, and would be only pe-
ripherally interested in what happened to outsiders. Jonah
did not want God to show compassion on Gentile Nineveh.
Jonah felt divine love and grace should be reserved for his
own "tribe." Jonah's god was too small. His narrow mind
did not reflect spiritual maturity (see Jonah 1:3).

Like Jonah, many church members today subscribe to
the notion of a tribalistic god. Missionary zeal is on the decline, even in traditional missions-minded church groups
and denominations. Leaders and followers want more for
local purposes, more for building the home church, more
for themselves and more for their communities. But Christianity holds, and should hold, larger generosity than that.
Sometimes Christians in local situations argue that to give
more to the local work and less to the outer mission will
improve the local congregation so that in the future it will
contribute more to missions. But such congregations sel-

dom follow through on those intentions. Their argument becomes an excuse for self-interest, and a reason for losing the vision for world missions.

Maturing believers will be doing something meaningful about the Great Commission of Jesus. Christianity is not a tribal religion. Anyone believing in less than world scope for the message of Christ is not projecting a biblical pattern. Jonah tried to make God over, and from what we know about Jonah, he did not finish well. If our analysis is justified, Jonah was not spiritually mature.

In the New Testament, one of Jesus' disciples, Judas, insisted on forming a political/social god. Judas would rather sell a costly perfume and use the profit to feed the poor than use it in the worship of the Son of God (see John 12:3-8). Judas' purpose was likely political, not related to concern for the needs of the poor. He was more likely concerned with making a political statement than showing compassion for the poor. Perhaps Judas thought he would win power for himself by providing benefit for citizens.

Like many political figures, Judas would use this Jesus religion, or any other workable one, to win his purpose. Whether the religion was right or wrong made little difference. For him, the object was social—how to make earthly life the good life, and how to reward himself in the making. Although Judas started at Jesus' side in the best of possible circumstances, he did not finish well because he decided to make God over in a political image.

The apostle Paul's friend, Demas, preferred a God who fit well in an affluent world. Scripture says Demas "loved this world," and accordingly deserted Paul in prison and headed on to the city of Thessalonica (see 2 Timothy 4:10). Perhaps he wondered if helping Paul would diminish his status in the affluent pagan world. He may have blamed Paul for being so overzealous and stupid as to get himself into such a fix. For Demas, the apostle seemed too radical—an embarrassment to the emerging "mainline" Christians. The biblical record implies that Demas did not finish well. Demas decided to make God over to fit into a comfortable culture. Demas has his followers to this day, people who may appear to be attractive but are spiritually immature.

Many men and women attempt to remake God. Perhaps the worst distortion of all comes from those who remake God in their own images. Powerful, arrogant Herod Agrippa, grandson of Herod the Great, ultimately became so convinced of his own worth that he allowed his subjects to call him a "god." But his delusions did not last long. Luke pungently reported: "Immediately, because Herod did not give praise to God, an angel of the Lord struck him down, and he was eaten by worms and died" (Acts 12:23).

Herod did not finish well because he did not finish as a responsible human leader. More importantly, he finished poorly because he was in human costume, a man masquerading as God. Herod thought that he could make God over in Herod's image. Preposterous. His fantasy came from an undeveloped and immature mind.

Our own experiences and thinking incorporate the way we revise God and His ways. Like the men of old, we may be presumptuous to try to amend God's purpose and program. There are many ways we can "remake" God to suit our own ideas.

A modern creation is a permissive and grandfatherly God, as illustrated in an article in a national newspaper about a movie queen recovering from illness. The actress, not known for righteousness, nonetheless acknowledged God's involvement during her life-threatening illness. The article refers to her passion for "cheeseburgers" and "her husky live-in lover, . . . 20 years her junior. . . ." Married seven times, she stated, according to the report, "I don't think I'll ever get married again." Describing her illness with "earthly humor," the actress reported she felt "great warmth." She said, "I was filled with love, and I remember saying, 'Thank you, God, thank you, God.' I knew I would live—without asking for it." She then said, "I'm actually very connected to the spiritual experience . . . to God."

The article continues: "She lives like any wealthy, busy Bel Air matron: '. . . I watch TV, go to the movies, go for drives, for picnics, play with my animals. . . . I just live a normal, quiet life, go to friends' houses for dinner, to see a movie—most of my friends have projection rooms.' " She attends Alcoholics Anonymous, and, because of lung disorders, avoids tobacco, even rooms where others are smoking. About giving up cigarettes she is quoted as saying, "Oh God, it's awful! I'm getting so pure. Thank God there are one or two things left. Yes, sex is one, but that's not sinful."[2] (Shortly after the interview was reported, she married her lover.)

Like the actress, we too can become nominalists in our interpretation of Scripture and life. The nominalist knows the right words and even some of the right ideas, but translates neither into right action. For nominalists the great moral ideas, including God, have small place in the reality of human conduct. When Europeans emigrate to the United States or Canada, they report a different perception than their culture advances. Many are surprised to discover that North American Christians believe that faith should be translated into daily living. They claim that in Europe, Christianity is believed in theory but left to some ephemeral place with meaning for the individual at death. It becomes a faith of acknowledgment, but not of life. Their god is more theoretical than practical. Such a god does not inspire worship.

There are other ways of "making over" God. We may dabble in immorality. We know God is not given to retribution, so we may create a god who becomes highly permissive for anything we wish to incorporate into life. With that belief, we feel safe in doing whatever we choose to do, even if it violates scriptural directives and troubles our consciences. A conscience can be cauterized.

An effective young evangelist went on to become an effective middle-aged evangelist, except that he also became a womanizer. In the early 1980s he was found out. He justified himself to his wife by saying that what he did must have been all right because: "God blesses my ministry." The evangelist, demonstrating monumental immaturity, had made up his own god. As far as he was concerned, God is a god who looks away from sin so long as the sinner is preaching the Word. He forgot that Scripture is the coin of the realm, and is legal tender no matter who uses it, that it is possible to preach without a genuine spiritual connection. Paul recognized this danger when he wrote, "I beat my body and make it my slave so that after I have preached to others, I myself will not be disqualified for the prize" (1 Corinthians 9:27).

Correction can be made in one's theology and practice. King Manasseh is an example of a man who had lived most of his life presuming on what he believed to be a permissive God, if there was a God at all, but who turned his life around in later years.

Manasseh reigned as king of Judah after Hezekiah (see 2 Chronicles 33). He ruled longer than any other Judaic king— 55 years. He began his reign with an energetic attempt to destroy the memory of Jehovah, followed by rebuilding pagan altars for Baal and establishing the Asherim. He even prostituted the temple altar by erecting a carved idol there. Manasseh forced his sons to pass through fire, practiced witchcraft and sorcery, and dealt favorably with mediums and spiritists. Scripture judges Manasseh's evil as worse than that of the wicked nations Israel had displaced.

The king of Assyria attacked Israel, captured Manasseh, and took him in chains and with a thong through his nose to Babylon. Manasseh made a dramatic change in faith and conduct. Humbled, he repented, and the Lord caused him to be returned to Jerusalem where he labored to undo what he had so arrogantly done. Although unable to erase totally the buildup of his early years, he did restore the Lord's altar and called Israel to worship with the sacrifices ordained by the Mosaic law. Manasseh's turnaround was remarkable.

It is important to say that even though Manasseh left consequences in the kingdom that could not be fully absolved, he personally finished well.

Although we are subject to all of the same barriers to maturity as our biblical counterparts, we can find hope for upward movement in spiritual maturation as we wait on the Lord for His grace, His strength, His faith. Isaiah 40:31 (NASB) offers encouragement for those who want to finish well:

> "Yet those who wait for the LORD" (they endure),
> "Will gain new strength;" (they are spiritually empowered),
> "They will mount up with wings like eagles," (they find strength to mature),
> "They will run and not get tired," (they persist to finish well) and
> "They will walk and not become weary" (they find steady growth).

What biblical examples are there of men and women who finished well? Scripture does not detail biographies of persons who finished their courses earning the epitaph, "Well done." That studied omission may relate to common negative reaction. We do not like to make comparisons and contrasts with affirmative achievers. This is not only the pattern of Scripture but appears in secular literature as well. For example, most published material about marriage is developed, not from successful marriages, but dysfunctional. Writers refer to "the sparse literature on happy marriages." We are more comfortable identifying with faltering men and women.

The apostle Paul wrote about the problem: "For we are not bold to class or compare oursleves with some of those who commend themselves; but when they measure themselves by themselves, and compare themselves with themselves, they are without understanding" (2 Corinthians

10:12, NASB). The apostle ended the statement by referring to the Christian standard of commendation — "whom
the Lord recommends." From the beginning, the ideal appears to have been, that in all matters the criteria for gaining the recommendation of the Lord is found in the
teachings of Scripture. Significant among those teachings
is that devout persons make Christ their model, in word
and deed.

The New Testament primarily accents principles, especially as they are modeled in Jesus, and stipulated in the
Epistles. The expectation is that, based on the divine narrative and Example, persons may, in faith, cultivate their special lives, finishing out well. The scriptural assertion is that
individuals should not be cast into merely human molds.
That hosts of men and women have finished well cannot be
denied when passages like Hebrews 11 are studied in their
implications. This summary chapter alone provides a list
longer than any grouping of Bible characters who failed.
Inclusion in the list for any man or woman would be honorable epitaph. The list included names of persons we perceive did not finish well, but the accent of the chapter is on
faith, not excellence of life performance. Nevertheless, it
does provide the strong implication that effective life resources to the end of human experience are desirable and
possible.

The Bible only summarizes, in sketchy passages, the biographies of 300 to 400 persons. Some of these who appear
to have finished well were: Melchizedek, Abraham, Joseph
in Egypt, Jethro, Joshua, a few kings of Judah, Abigail,
Mordecai and Esther, Isaiah, Daniel and his three friends,
Nehemiah, Mary and Joseph, Stephen, Barnabas, the apostles Paul, Peter, James and John, Aquila and Priscilla,
Timothy and Titus and scores of others. They were followed by admirable apostolic and church fathers. History
informs little of the masses from which clouds of effective
witnesses lived out their lives to maturity and death.

In more recent history, since those ancient times of magnificent saints, the stories of hosts of eminent and obscure Christians and their works have repeated the principles of effective living, related to growing maturity, to life's end. Not only have stories of devout and mature laymen and clergy been told, persons like Jonathan Edwards, Mother Teresa, and others, like Billy Graham, but the organizations they founded or served have extended them. From the Graham organization, Harvey Mackay recommended to business executives: ". . . show a little appreciation. Every year the Billy Graham organization holds an annual luncheon honoring its suppliers. Every one of us troops over to their building and gets a round of applause and a much needed spiritual lift. It's good ministering and it's good business. Which is one reason why they're the best there is at what they do." [3]

General society does not know how to evaluate the Christian experience, although society holds a deep-down feeling that to be genuine in Christian life must be a very great thing. The reality seems elusive to them, even impossible. It's like a fairy tale. They continue in secular evaluation, which the apostle deplored to the Corinthians. Illustrations of secularism are commonplace. When it was discovered that persons who "blessed their food" were healthier than those who did not, the conclusion of the researchers was not that God did indeed bless the food, but delay in eating occasioned by prayer, meant a more relaxed attitude which served better digestion for the diners. That both blessing and natural benefit may be mutual accompaniments was not suggested.

Finding conservative Christians (as compared to liberal Christians and secularists) were more gratified in their conjugal relationships with their mates, observers concluded that devout Christians were doing something they perceived to be a bit "naughty" so were animated above those accepting sex as normal, therefore ordinary. (The liberal Christians, it was also discovered, were happier with the intimacy of their marriages than were the secularists, but not so gratified as the conservative group). Could the satisfaction be related to greater acceptance of the limits of human sexuality on the part of religious persons than nonreligious? That possibility was not forwarded among the conclusions. And other logical possibilities were also passed over. (Liberal Christian voices have addressed the business of maturity and morality in affirmative ways. Note the matter of politics in Jim Wallis' book, *The Soul of Politics*).

When it was discovered that Christians live longer, vote more often, have better educational performances, enjoy more committed marriages and practice other beneficial habits, the conclusions did not attribute faith in God, or God Himself, as cause for these conducts. The results were usually credited to some natural consequence, and even then, the published findings were passed over. Secular sources generally disregarded those results in any recommendations for social improvement. Where is hoped-for objectivity?

To find the meaning of Christianity in personal progress toward finishing well, the following chapters of this book are presented. They appear as the result of a lifetime of biblical studies. From Scripture is found the Christian criteria for evaluation and source of understanding, wisdom and knowledge for how life ought to be lived. The ideas also grow out of observation of Christians and non-Christians in everyday life, of laymen and clergy, in the United States, Canada and overseas.

That there are persons, seldom heralded, who have finished well, needs to be affirmed. They personified, as I got to know a few of them and saw some of them die, the concepts of the Scripture that commend good and mature men and women. What does Scripture have to say about completion—about finishing well? The Apostle Paul apparently discovered the answer:

If we endure we will also reign with him. (2 Timothy 2:12)

For I am already being poured out like a drink offering, and the time has come for my departure. I have fought the good fight, I have finished the race, I have kept the faith. Now there is in store for me the crown of righteousness, which the Lord, the righteous Judge, will award to me on that day—and not only to me, but also to all who have longed for his appearing. (2 Timothy 4:6-8)

But I do not consider my life of any account as dear to myself, in order that I may finish my course, and the ministry which I received from the Lord Jesus, to testify solemnly of the gospel of the grace of God. (Acts 20:24, NASB)

The principle is accented in the words of One dying at 33 years of age: "It is finished." What was finished? The purpose of His life, the character, the integrity, the wisdom, had all been lived out and communicated. Crucifixion, the manner of Jesus' death, was not, and is not, the criteria of success or failure for His life on earth, as society might perceive the event. But that sacrifice was entirely related to the completed story of a unique offering of God for mankind. It speaks to devout Christian men and women everywhere relative to their own lives and deaths, and how they wished they had lived. It speaks also to the skeptic, the profane and all others.

Endnotes

1 "The Mystery of Measuring Ministry." A Leadership Forum. Roberts, Martin, Martin, Aldrich. *Leadership*, Summer 1992, p. 134.

2 Williams, Jeannie. "After brush with death 'I'm happy,' " *USA Today*, November 20, 1990, pp. A1-A2. Copyright 1990, USA Today. Reprinted by permission.

3 Mackay, Harvey. "For Executives Only," *Minneapolis Star-Tribune*, May 18, 1995, p. 2-D. Copyright 1995, United Feature Syndicate, all rights reserved. Reprinted by permission.

_____ *Chapter*

_____ *3*

Step Up to Maturity

It was he who gave some to be apostles, some to be prophets, some to be evangelists, and some to be pastors and teachers, to prepare God's people for works of service, so that the body of Christ may be built up until we all reach unity in the faith and in the knowledge of the Son of God and become mature, attaining to the whole measure of the fullness of Christ.

Then we will no longer be infants, tossed back and forth by the waves, and blown here and there by every wind of teaching and by the cunning and craftiness of men in their deceitful scheming. Instead, speaking the truth in love, we will in all things grow up into him who is the Head, that is, Christ. From him the whole body, joined and held together by every supporting ligament, grows and builds itself up in love, as each part does its work. (Ephesians 4:11-16)

Although most men and women have not articulated a definition of maturity, they perceive the value of becoming mature. When college students responded to a poll asking what qualities they believed to be necessary for their personal lives, maturity was the

most commonly given answer. Although maturity was
not defined for or by these students, they used the word
with approval.

In responding to questions about the meaning of maturity, persons have all kinds of answers from "growing old"
to "managing money responsibility" to "sticking at one's
tasks" to "living above anger" and the like. Each person
seems to have his or her own twist about the meaning of
maturity. Most seem to feel it is an escape from puberty or
the advancement into old age.

The writer to the Hebrews accented maturity by con-
trasting it with immaturity in the Christian context:
"milk" for the immature, but "solid food" for the mature.
The immature require repetition of "elementary truths,"
but the mature can "distinguish good from evil" (5:12-14).
The immature remain dull; therefore they must repeat fundamentals, and so are slow learners. The mature, by pro-
gressing, are capable or becoming "teachers." They are able
to instruct others.

Definitions for maturity will vary, but there are certain
concepts about which everyone can agree. For example, most
persons agree that maturity is not childishness or adolescence.
Maturity has inherent in it connotations of personal excellence and virtue. No single definition includes everything en-
compassed in maturity, but it is profitable to consider some of
the ways this important word has been defined.

Gordon W. Alport, a Harvard psychologist who special-
ized in the study of personality traits, provided a more
theoretical definition. Alport said the mature person is
characterized by the following six qualities:

1. He is self-critical, providing his own design for self-improvement;
2. He is self-motivated, driving himself onward;
3. He is consistent in his moral choices, understanding
their consequences;
4. He is able to respond to a broad range of life issues;

5. He is integrated in his personality; and
6. He is heuristic in his approach to learning, building upon previous growth.

William James, before Alport, was somewhat broader, almost spiritual, in his definition and description of the mature person:
1. He has a feeling he is dwelling in a larger life than would otherwise be the case;
2. He has a sense of the continuity of the friendly power of his own life;
3. He has an awareness of immense elation and freedom; and
4. He has a shift of his emotional center toward loving and harmonious affections.

While these human definitions offer much with which Christians can readily agree, there is more, much more, to spiritual maturity. Christian maturity is the ultimate in spiritual growth, transcending maturity defined in secular terms.

Christian maturity is marked by a thoroughgoing Christlikeness in character, attitudes and conduct. It is formed by divine wisdom, and is attained through moral growth that includes the believer's full integrity. It manifests itself in humility, patience, grace and power—characteristics not measurable in scientific terms. Christian maturity is real and felt, readily observed in its practice. There is immortality in it. This chapter begins the search for Christian maturity.

Maturity Goes Beyond Rudimentary Understanding

Therefore let us leave the elementary teachings about Christ and go on to maturity, not laying again the foundation of repentance from acts that lead to death, and of faith in God, instruction

about baptisms, the laying on of hands, the resurrection of the dead, and eternal judgment. And
God permitting, we will do so. (Hebrews 6:1-3)

The writer to the Hebrews began his teaching on maturity by informing the reader what it is not. Maturity is not
the repetition, in thought and practice, of fundamental
truths. He wrote that there are certain teachings that mature persons have already learned—elementary teachings
that are basic to the process of evangelism, teachings that
are rudimentary to the Christian faith.

There is elementary teaching about Jesus Christ. This elementary teaching encompasses the other six basic teachings outlined in these verses. The elementary teaching
about Jesus Christ calls for dynamic (life-changing) faith
that Christ came from God. It includes, among other issues, an understanding of the person of Jesus Christ, and
the story of human redemption by His personal sacrifice.
Such teaching is vital to Christianity. It includes the historical Jesus who was born, lived, died, and was resurrected
in Palestine.

Believing and understanding the elementary truths of
Christ are as important to ongoing Christian faith as learning to read and write is to a person's later education and
development. When the fundamentals of reading and writing have been learned and mastered, one need not continue
exclusive study of those skills, but may utilize them for further learning. Even though the skills are honed as they are
used, they become means to other ends. Likewise, early in
the formative Christian experience the believer should gain
a clear, elementary concept of biblical Christology. It is basic to all that follows.

But as we look at churches in our generation and culture,
we get the feeling that the majority of Christians may be
preoccupied with the rudiments of their faith. Pastors and
authors are steered away from deeper issues. Preachers are
often requested to hold to shortened homilies, and are

asked to repeat, in some interesting context of course, the basic evangel and a few favorite sacred phrases. By the same token, substantive material is not easily sold in Christian publishing. Books dealing with profound teachings for Christian living are neglected, while books that incorporate "interesting stories," especially autobiographies of persons who received God's deliverance in unusual or tragic experiences, sell rapidly.

The writer to the Hebrews was concerned with these kinds of issues. He urged readers to get on with teachings subsequent to salvation. He did not say that the fundamentals should be forgotten or neglected, but that they should be balanced with teaching on Christian growth. He proceeded to outline six basic truths that make up elementary doctrine about Christian life and beliefs.

Repentance is elementary. Repentance is the road each person travels if he or she is to become a Christian in the biblical order of salvation. Repentance involves a sorrow for personal sin that motivates individuals to acknowledge themselves sinners. Initially, repentance is to God, who hears this sincere confession of the human soul. But later the person also asks forgiveness of persons sinned against, and makes restitution wherever possible. Making restitution in the cases where the offenses require it contributes to assurance of forgiveness.

Dead works are elementary. It is necessary that every believer understand that "dead works" are ineffective for generating salvation. Salvation from sin is not gained by any human accomplishment or by the performance of good deeds. Human virtue, as important as it is for decency, has no lasting redemptive quality. The writer to the Hebrews was not suggesting that works are unimportant, only that they are impotent to achieve salvation.

Faith in God is elementary. Although human beings generally seek to verify their knowledge through sensory experience—to touch, see, hear, smell or taste what they claim to know—spiritual truth, at least the greater part of it, must become experience through faith. Faith is a necessary complement to repentance for salvation, and is also evidence that the individual is not relying on his or her good conduct (dead works) to gain salvation.

Personal sophistication is not necessary for exercising spiritual faith. A simpleton may grasp faith, while a scholar may miss it totally. The Greeks made intellectual prowess the measure of a person's quality, but Israel was tested by morality. Morality depends on faith because people, recognizing their own moral inability, must trust in God's provision to make up for the lack.

Instruction about procedures is elementary. New converts need to receive instruction about the orthodox meanings of foundational Christian ordinances like baptism and communion; they need to learn effective approaches to spiritual disciplines like praying and seeking biblical truth. An understanding and application of these truths ought to be evident in the lives of young Christians as early as possible.

Instruction about death is elementary. Immortality is a truth that is key to understanding Christian salvation. A specific belief in life after death is part of the motivation of the gospel. One should conduct oneself differently in everyday experience when one realizes that human life is transitional rather than terminal. The gate to God's presence is death. The Christian should understand that physical death will ultimately be set aside by physical resurrection and that this present life, therefore, holds meaning for the next. He or she knows that Christians will ultimately stand, in the flesh, in the presence of God.

Eternal judgment is elementary. Here, the gospel is communicated in terms of what happens when it is slighted. It is basic to understand that genuine acceptance of the gospel means blessed immortality—an affirmation of life. It is equally basic to understand that rejection of the gospel means eternal judgment—a negation of life. Eternal judgment, an everlasting consciousness away from God, is stated as a motivational force for witnessing. The apostle

Paul affirmed that God has "terror" in Him (2 Corinthians 5:11, KJV), and that knowledge of His terror is part of the reason Christians should persuade men and women to seek salvation.

After the writer to the Hebrews covered the elementary teachings, but before he moved into the subject of maturity, he gave a solemn warning, one which is not easily understood but which demands attention, if for no other reason than that it appears in the serious context of this passage in Hebrews 6.

Apostasy (vss. 4-6) Can a person become a Christian, and by a subsequent rejection of his experience, become apostate? Whole theological theories have turned on the answer to that question. A person might sense contradictions as he deals with the issue, but he can also sense the providence of God. In any event, the concepts of "perseverance" and "endurance to the end" have strong meaning to the Christian seeking maturity. The mature Christian lasts. He or she prevails. There is a difference, for example, in the lives of Peter and Judas, who both were characterized, during Jesus' earthly ministry, as followers and believers of Christ. The mature Christian cannot become apostate (2 Peter 1:10).

With all that said, the writer to the Hebrews finished out chapter six with instruction on those factors which encourage spiritual growth and ministry.

Hope (vss. 11, 18-19) Hope, in the biblical context, is more than most Christians perceive it to be. While many sermons, poems and songs have been written about faith and love, few are written about hope as it is meant to be understood in the biblical equation. Hope understands that ultimately God will make right everything that has ever been wrong. Hope counts on the continuing future of the believer. Hope puts time in its place. Hope means all ends well, and all will be made right (see Romans 12:12).

Perseverance (vs. 11) Endurance is, as discussed elsewhere in this writing, a significant test of genuine Christian experience. It is one of the ultimate tests. Enduring to the end (see Matthew 10:22) gives people a clear measure of themselves to themselves, and of themselves to God. One of the minister's principle duties is to preach and teach the ramifications of this biblical truth in order for developing Christians to become and remain resolute. In some way this perseverance of faith relates to an opposite option, apostasy, as referred to above. Perseverance is consistent performance, evidence to oneself of his authority over his own will. Perseverance overcomes boredom and fatigue as well as doubt, and therefore fortifies faith.

Patience (v. 12) Scripture repeatedly teaches the concept of Christian patience. It is a factor underlying much of what is Christian—it is necessary for humility, for faith, for the practice of mature Christian life. Its greatest test, however, is to believe that Christ will return, no matter how long He delays that return. A Christian's genuine desire for and growing conviction about the return of Jesus Christ are evidences of maturity and growth in spiritual perception. Sometimes persons begin to doubt when it becomes clear that the promised event will not take place as soon as they had believed. Scripture refers to this kind of impatience relative to Christ's return as a sign of immaturity (2 Peter 3:4). Patience leading to maturity is different from perseverance (patience with time and self), and is more related to spiritual acceptance (patience with God and God's plan). Patience also puts time in its place. (Note Lamentations 3:24-26.)

Models (v. 12) A Christian's conduct, observable by family members, colleagues, believers and unbelievers, gives the overall impression of that person's Christian experience. To follow Christ in daily belief and conduct is a major injunction the apostle repeatedly stressed. The Model (Christ) makes models (Paul being one).

Immature persons do not make satisfactory models, and often do not want to become models, even though they expect model conduct in others. Mature persons do not look for models so much as they mean to become models. Modeling is basic to learning; learners need examples, so excellent teachers become models, even if inadvertently. The adult who rejects the responsibility of his own modeling also rejects maturity to some degree.

One rightly wonders what or how one is to model. People are best when they find the wholeness of the Christian experience. Peter Kreeft raised the issue in the analogy of strong bones and firm flesh, the evidence of physical maturity:

> So in waging spiritual warfare we must avoid both the ancient, "hard" mistake and the modern, "soft" mistake. Our ancestors were better than we are at the "hard" virtues, like courage and chastity. We are better at the "soft" virtues, like kindness and philanthropy. But you can no more specialize in virtue than in anatomical organs. The virtues are like organs in a body; interdependent. Compassion without courage ceases under pressure, and compassion without justice is wasted. Justice without mercy becomes cruelty; chastity without charity, coldness. The "hard" virtues are like the bones in a body, and the "soft" virtues like tissues. Bones without tissues are a skeleton; tissues without bones, a jellyfish.[1]

Faith (v. 12) Faith appears in both lists of topics in the Hebrews account—lists of both elementary and maturity factors. Elementary faith makes salvation generative. Mature faith is necessary for growth into the fully furnished person in Christ. Faith is rudimentary, but also progressive. It grows, even feeling different to the maturing Christian than does elementary faith. It is a line running through all matters pertaining to God and people.

Mature faith maintains growth as it helps the Christian in making God personal, prayer effective, and life bearable, even joyful. Because it is by faith that God does His work for and through the Christian, faith is as vital in later growth and experience as it is in earlier. As oxygen is necessary for physical life both in babes and the elderly, so Christian faith is universally necessary for every stage of spiritual life.

Maturity Grows with the Practice of Spiritual Gifts

Ephesians 4:11-16, which introduced this chapter, gives a list of ministerial gifts that are, or ought to be, used for the purpose of developing mature believers and accomplishing ministry. In this passage the apostle refers not only to clergy, but to all Christians who seek maturity and appropriate service to God. Maturity is involved with service that builds up the Church. Through unity of faith and knowledge of Christ, believers grow to full stature.

The serving Christian needs divine gifts to perform the special creative tasks of nourishing and exercising Christians toward maturity. As, humanly speaking, some persons possess talents that make them more than ordinarily effective in certain things they do, so Christians are provided spiritual gifts to qualify them to serve at higher than ordinary levels.

There is analogy in the patterns of everyday life. The medical profession commonly divides physicians into general practitioners and specialists. The first accents the health of the whole body; the second, one of its parts or systems. The Church has specialists in its several ministries. The objective, of course, relates ultimately to the health of the whole body.

The Church needs persons gifted in the areas in which Christian growth is expected. Scripture describes the gifts of apostles, prophets, evangelists, pastors, teachers and others prepared for special purposes. These men and women effectively nurture Christian believers. Some of them use special gifts to win believers, while others disciple those believers in their spiritual growth.

The "evangelist" mentioned in this passage deserves closer examination. Since witnessing is an evangelistic activity involving all Christians, why is "evangelist" included here with the other gifts? The evangelist edifies and challenges the Church for witness. Often this leads to the renewal and revival of those long since evangelized.

While it is true that all Christians ought to communicate their faith, those gifted as evangelists gain larger results than those without this special gift. Their effective witness becomes a model to those who lack the specific enabling. Examples of men with the gift of evangelism are Dwight L. Moody and Billy Graham.

Usually, the gifted evangelists are formal presenters of Christian salvation. They win, through their communication, more persons to faith in Christ than those who do not possess an evangelistic gift. The difference between the one with the evangel's gift and the lay witness may be likened to the difference between the finger painter and Rembrandt, between the sandlot player and Joe DiMaggio, between the church layman and Jonathan Edwards or Billy Graham. The layman witnesses, Graham evangelizes. The layman succeeds with one or a few; the gifted evangelist, with many.

Before moving away from his discussion on the areas of gifted service, the apostle paused to comment about influences that were impeding the Ephesians' spiritual growth. These immature ones were "tossed back and forth by the waves," (Ephesians 4:14) and, as the Greek text casts the idea, "duped by crafty rogues and their deceitful schemes."

The descriptive image of tossing is also apt for the current generation. Christians who require constant emotional elation in order to feel that they are spiritually fulfilled are on tossing waves. These persons believe that an absence of emotional highs is evidence of spiritual decline or failure. They are easily thrown when interpersonal problems interfere in Christian fellowships.

As for the crafty rogues with deceitful schemes, some ministers, we know, represent themselves and Christ unsatisfactorily. One author described the experiment he performed on one of these charlatans:

> A recent mass mailing from the . . . Association in Phoenix invited me to use a convenient clip-out form to check my desired miracle. . . . The Association was directed by a media minister.
>
> One of his mailings enclosed a "miracle prayer cloth" which had touched his body. . . . Monetary offerings are, of course . . . encouraged. . . .
>
> I decided to test the . . . miracle system: I asked this "man of cloth" to get God "to stop the man from exploiting suffering people with his arrogant self-deification." A week later, right on schedule, my prayer cloth returned along with a letter (printed to appear handwritten) in which the man assured me that "for 3 days and 3 nights your special prayer requests and prayer cloth have been in my private prayer chamber and I've been praying. I've asked God to give you this special miracle to put His hand on your loved one. I really feel good about it! Victory is coming."[2]

The writer reported, regrettably, that the promised miracle had not yet occurred, as the man continued on the air at the time of his writing. The prayer request—a request for the preacher's own decline, was apparently never read.

We are embarrassed about these false religious practitioners, and if we are mature, we look for ways to treat the problem without undermining genuine ministry. The Ephesian epistle dealt with two groups of people who were potentially stalled in their Christian growth by this situation: the tricksters themselves, and those who are taken in by their craftiness and deceitfulness. The apostle Paul wrote that those who are susceptible to such schemes are not mature spiritual adults, but children. When believers "grow up" in applied faith, they avoid such pitfalls.

Maturity Means a Different Way of Thinking

But whatever was to my profit I now consider loss for the sake of Christ. What is more, I consider everything a loss compared to the surpassing greatness of knowing Christ Jesus my Lord, for whose sake I have lost all things. I consider them rubbish, that I may gain Christ and be found in him, not having a righteousness of my own that comes from the law, but that which is through faith in Christ—the righteousness that comes from God and is by faith. I want to know Christ and the power of his resurrection and the fellowship of sharing in his sufferings, becoming like him in his death, and so, somehow, to attain to the resurrection from the dead.

Not that I have already obtained all this, or have already been made perfect, but I press on to take hold of that for which Christ Jesus took hold of me. Brothers, I do not consider myself yet to have taken hold of it. But one thing I do: Forgetting what is behind and straining toward what is ahead, I press on toward the goal to win the prize for which God has called me heavenward in Christ Jesus.

All of us who are mature should take such a view of things. And if on some point you think differently, that too God will make clear to you. Only let us live up to what we have already attained. (Philippians 3:7-16)

The word "perfect" in the above quotation comes from the Greek *teleio*, which is a verb meaning "to be complete, or to accomplish, or to consummate a character, or to be perfect." It refers to consecrating, to finishing, to fulfilling the character. It is an ultimate goal toward which the Christian should be making progress. The word "mature" in the passage is translated from the related Greek word *teleios*, which is an adjective defining the Christian and referring to completion in the context of mental and moral character. It means completeness to the full moral age of a Christian man or woman.

Prior to his conversion, self-benefit and self-pride were prime motivators in Paul's life. As a rigid law-keeper in the legalistic orthodox religion, Paul tended toward pride. But after his conversion, those matters became like "rubbish" to him. His former orientation toward legalistic beliefs became unimportant, even troublesome, when he began to live in the accomplishments of Christ. The liberation of his new life stood in stark contrast to the legalism of his old life. (Note 2 Corinthians 10-12.)

At this point in the Philippian letter, the apostle related how he had chosen to drop his former thought patterns and to focus instead on the mature pattern of Christian thinking. Mature believers, the apostle affirmed, grow in their knowledge of Christ, and that knowledge includes their relationship to His suffering, death and resurrection (see Philippians 3:10). As believers fully identify with Christ in the knowledge and experience of His suffering and death, their faith prepares them for their own physical death and later resurrection triumph.

The apostle Paul acknowledged that he had not gained full spiritual stature during his human life. No one can. But a person can always be growing. The apostle did aspire to gain full spiritual stature insofar as possible. Mature persons reach beyond their grasp and in stretching they accomplish more objectives than they would resigning to gravity.

Steven Mosley, in his book *A Tale of Three Virtues*, rightly points out that "religious goodness" is conventionally perceived as avoidance of evils, perhaps stipulated evils having to do with uses of language, sex and various other human actions. Mosley found this concept to be intimidating, but unchallenging. He would have Christians re-imagine virtue with its first passion. In the new creation in Christ the believer makes righteousness "a consuming pursuit."[3] It is not circumcision or a series of taboos that are maintained, but an active life which is a creative expression, therefore an art. It goes beyond avoidance, and makes positive impact as it did with Paul and with a long line of saints and pilgrims.

Maturity Is for Every Christian

... Christ in you, the hope of glory.

And we proclaim Him, admonishing every man and teaching every man with all wisdom, that we may present every man complete in Christ.

And for this purpose also I labor, striving according to His power, which mightily works within me. (Colossians 1:27-29, NASB)

Christians were admonished to be "complete" in Christ. We cannot escape noticing how Paul repeatedly uses the word "every." All Christians are included in this admonition; none are exempt.

"Complete" *(teleios)* in this passage is another English word representing maturity. The reference here is not to the theological concept of justification although justification is basic to it. It refers instead to a growing experience for every Christian.

The focus of this text is not on maturity itself, but on the means to it—the ministry of Christ in the believer. As we have seen, maturity is addressed and developed in other Bible texts. In this text it is assumed. The meaning here is that maturity is for every living Christian, and that the apostle's ministry was dedicated and organized for accomplishing that purpose. Paul proclaimed that maturity is an expected, and therefore possible, Christian experience which is—or ought to be—standard for all believers.

Because of this truth we face perhaps one of the largest disappointments in the life of the Church. Many believers stop short of their full potential in Christ; their spiritual lives are underdeveloped and incomplete. Observers from within the Church, as well as from without, acknowledge this lack of growth in church members as a general scandal.

There are myriad reasons why Christians fail to mature. There are negative attitudes—bitterness, anger, rudeness, over-aggressiveness, narcissism, depression based on spiritual distortions.

There are carnal habits—prayerlessness, inappropriate language, materialism, immorality, alcohol and drug abuse, questionable recreational activities.

There is irresponsibility in relationships—family breakdowns, accusation and gossip, omission of duty, church disruption and neglect, lack of sufficient social concern.

In addition, the Church has its own problems—general doubt, apathy, creeping heresies, disobedience to known biblical directives, aberrations of righteous conduct. The ultimate result is registered in the dropout level of men and women from the Church.

These negative factors, and many others besides, put an obvious strain on the Church. It is becoming more difficult to defend strongly a church that teaches so magnificent a truth and way of life, but whose members practice lifestyles significantly inferior to these teachings. Adherents in other faiths often seem more dedicated than some Christians, a matter which received serious discussion around the world in 1990 when Iraq invaded Kuwait. Faithful Moslems willingly gave up comforts, freedoms, even life, for their belief in Allah. There was no shortage of Moslem volunteers for suicide squads, while those who refused to serve Allah were labeled "satanic" and deemed worthy of scorn and death. In contrast, most Americans who discussed the matter in the news media did not perceive anything worth dying for prematurely.

Accordingly, there arises the feeling that the Christian Church, and by implication, Christ, cannot deliver in reality what is promised in theory. If He could, it would seem His followers would live their lives in faithfulness to His teachings. But Christ cannot be faulted, and faithful believers know that. Responsibility rests, instead, on church members. American culture, even among churchgoers, acts like there is little in which to believe.

Part of the problem may be the emerging evangelical culture. The banality of the popular culture seems to be making its way into the Church. Historically Christians have tried to express spiritual passion and reality in the arts—painting, sculpting, writing, building, speaking and making music. One is struck by the artistic quality of prayers that have been preserved in the writings of the centuries of saints. But concern for these cultural achievements is waning. We see the results in matters like church music that is casual and overly simple, and sermons that are kept basic, often redundant, for the excuse that unbelievers may be present. Issues are sometimes dished out as religious pabulum. Steven Mosley stated, "For Christian virtue to rise above its pale and monotonous image, it must, like art, become a bridge between the visible and the invisible."[4]

But a shallow evangelical culture is not the only problem—converts are won despite its shallowness. So the issue becomes who will help them build on their spiritual beginnings? Pastors can contribute to their flock's immaturity by failing to cultivate their own spiritual lives. They may not have grown in their own faith and knowledge to a point where they can deal effectively with substantive concepts. Ministers ought to be able to accomplish both the birthing and the nurturing assignments. It is argued that no other profession appears to have the number of rapid shifts in professional life as do ministers in their early and middle years. Pastors are trained for entering the ministry, but they are not always trained to *intensify* the ministry—to go "further up and further in," as C.S. Lewis once said. Many ministers are dissatisfied. Some drop out. Others are dropped. There is a surplus of ordained clergy, yet many pulpits are unfilled.

Ministers often attribute the problem to burnout, but that can be a misnomer. Some alleged burnout is really boredom or hypochondria. The apostle Paul, and many who have ministered in centuries after him, seemed little acquainted with burnout, for which we can be grateful. Most moderns would have a short list of sufferings compared to the apostle's—they simply would not be able to accept the rigors of apostolic ministry. Did former generations have greater hardiness than we? If they were sustained by the Holy Spirit, why cannot this generation be sustained by the same Holy Spirit?

In the study of any field or profession, including church history, we discover that the more mature the person, the more likely he or she was able to labor without succumbing to burnout, collapse or boredom. Mature persons discover ways to remain energized. They balance hard work with recreation. They know something about diet and physical regimens, including rest and exercise. They listen to the "sounds" of their bodies and respond to them appropriately—without becoming engrossed in themselves. Mature persons neither aspire to unattainable professional recognition, nor do they waste their energies on peripheral matters. Mature, healthy persons pace their lives. They design their life goals in accordance with their circumstances, talents, gifts and nature. They do things for others, and are energized in the doing. In balancing all of these considerations, they cultivate hardiness. Perhaps as much literature is needed on hardiness as is available on burnout and boredom.

There can be, of course, actual burnout. But burnout appears to be caused by circumstances over which most individuals have control. Sometimes ministers spend so much time and energy on others' spiritual lives and personal relationships that they neglect their own. Prayer may become cursory, and the Scriptures may become a source of sermon material rather than spiritual nourishment. As they shop the Bible for others, they overlook their own needs. They begin to ignore important personal matters, and as one thing leads to another, they neglect communication with their spouses, children, friends or colleagues. By this time deep distress sets in, and the energy for life, the will to prevail and the wisdom for self-help have all dissipated. These persons may pass the point of returning. We can take over as self problem-solvers, but it takes resolve.

A writer tells the story of an ancient language which included two characters, one standing for "heart" and the other for "head." The word "fool" was created by placing the "heart" character over the "head" character. The word "wisdom," as well as the word "king," placed the head over the heart. This is what the people sought in their king. For the Christian, the clarity and meaning of the spiritual mind is developed in various passages of Scripture, especially in the epistle to the Philippians. This "mind" leads to maturity.

Students of the subject of burnout say that it is more likely to occur in persons who are unhappy rather than happy. Unhappiness in people may be caused by the acts and attitudes of others as interpreted by those people, but it may be created by the people themselves. Often burnout is either alleged or caused in people as the result of unsatisfactory ways in which they psychologically "manage" others in their own attitudes and conduct. The burnout, or whatever negative thing it is that happens, should not occur as often as it does. In maturity people find mental health through their own moral improvements and satisfactory relationships with others. Developing people serve others and are served by them. They step up to maturity.

"Then we will no longer be infants. . . . Instead . . . grow up into him who is the Head, that is, Christ" (Ephesians 4:14-15).

Endnotes

1 Kreeft, Peter. "The Good War," *Christianity Today,* December 17, 1990, p. 31, quoting from Peter Kreeft's book, *Making Choices.*

2 Myers, David. *The Inflated Self* (New York: Seabury Press), pp. 138-139. Copyright 1980 by David Myers. Reprinted by permission of HarperCollins Publishers, Inc.

3 Mosley, Steven. "Dedalus's Complaint," *Christianity Today,* November 19, 1990, pp. 29-31. Adaptation of material from Steven Mosley's book, *A Tale of Three Virtues* (Sisters, Oregon: Questar, 1989).

4 Ibid.

_____ *Chapter*
_____ *4*

Signs of
Christian Maturity

Therefore let us, as many as are mature, have this mind;
and if in anything you think otherwise, God will reveal
even this to you. Nevertheless, to the degree we have al-
ready attained, let us walk by the same rule, let us be of
the same mind. (Philippians 3:15-16, NKJV)

Christians are not all equally mature. Some range in development is to be expected. Just as human beings progress physically from infancy, childhood, adolescence, adulthood to old age, so will Christians pass through various stages of spiritual development, beginning with salvation as a birthing experience, followed by growth to maturity. Spiritual maturity, like physical maturity, does not occur in an instant. Through no special effort of their own, most persons progress physically to old age, but Christians will not necessarily progress to spiritual prime. Spiritual growth requires sustained commitment. It is acknowledged that gradations also apply to immature persons, with some more immature than others.

In the previous chapter biblical maturity was defined broadly in terms of general beliefs and attitudes. In this chapter we will take a closer look at mature Christian attitudes and beliefs, but also explore some actions characterizing mature Christian experience.

The Mature Christian Lives a Life of Wholeness

The mature Christian does not overemphasize life-fragments. Small matters are not inflated out of proportion to other issues, and significant issues are not diminished. Separate experiences are not isolated as disjointed factors. Life is tied together in its parts. It is one piece, woven of all its parts, even from patches of minute experiences. Wholeness is extensive and an important biblical perception, especially related to the Church—"But now are they many members, yet but one body" (1 Corinthians 12:20, KJV). The principle of unity in God helps people understand their own wholeness, and the wholeness of people informs us in some way about God.

Knowledgeable Christians are spiritually holistic because they try to include all that is their life in their belief and conduct patterns. They know there are many links, not just one. How strong is the whole chain? The chain is important, and individual links important only as they are part of the chain. The separate parts, never unlinked, inform us about the whole. If any parts fail or are omitted, the whole is affected, even if only in a minimal way. But the reverse is also true, that if the stronger factors are called upon to assist in weak areas, the whole may be strengthened. The chain is not strung out between two competing forces. The chain is strengthened because it is wrapped.

The old aphorism about the chain and weakest link analogy is unsuitable for our purpose. People are stronger than the weakest point in their lives, as they are also weaker than their strongest. A lengthened chain is no stronger than its weakest link, but a chain wound around an object, as it often is in a mooring, draws upon other physical laws. It reinforces itself. A chain may be wound over itself and become strong enough to serve. Not all links in a life chain are strong enough on their own, but they may be made to hold with overlapping linkages.

Sin and righteousness are always at war in the person. Apparently each wins some battles. The separate battles, the skirmishes, are to be evaluated for what they are—single events tied into a life's large experience. Some events seem lost, except they provide experiences for the whole life that can lead careful persons to winning the next skirmish on that field.

Wholeness provides context for the interpretation of single events. Each tragedy, each benefit, each win, each loss, ought to be translated as much as possible in light of a whole life. Historians do not judge wars in terms of their battles, but they evaluate, at the end, the whole war as it relates to the scheme of history. Nevertheless, historians do study battles, primarily to find clues about the war. It is possible to win the battle and lose the war, as Pyrrhus discovered. The converse is also true, battles may be lost and the war won. Each matter needs to be evaluated in relation to all other matters. Both despair and exhilaration are often moderated when the full story is unfolded. Reality, not fantasy, is becoming to the mature person. Wholeness is reality.

Students of human behavior are impressed by "transcenders"—those who achieve effective lives even though they were given little in the way of nurture and resources. They tend to transcend impossible situations like abusive, drunken parents, especially when they find a model as a mentoring teacher or minister. Transcenders seem to leave their past, and focus on the future they mean to create into wholeness for themselves. Sociologists wonder about what it is that causes some youths to rise out of squalor and poor education to become effective, even princely, in their lives. Other persons start at average, or even less than average levels, flourish in midlife, and fade or hold even to the end of their professional careers. Some begin, start upward, and keep going upward as long as they maintain energy. The eminent persons who do elevate appear to have larger vision and mission for life than others.

Immature persons commonly fragment life, overemphasizing whatever is current in their activity. An event, by itself is easily overestimated. When it is, either elation or depression may result. Lives that are not "put together" suffer from distortions.

Mature Christians do not unduly accent this or that factor—an offense, a hurt or even a personal blessing. They cultivate an evenness in their lives which is, in itself, a blessing to them. That evenness is made dynamic by their mission. Mission, we have argued, is the common feature found in respected achievers. No other human factor appears more important than mission in evaluating greatness. The whole life concept is helpful in assisting a person to advance from lower plateaus, to elevated plateaus, and beyond to even higher plateaus. Each mature person should be able to answer well the questions: "What is my mission in life?" "How do I focus my life to gain my mission?"

The Mature Christian
Follows the Biblical Compass

The mature Christian can never accept secular humanism for direction. This person does not believe that humans are the measure of themselves much less of all things else. Consistent secular humanists hold that there is no one greater than humans to assist in their affairs. But like most points of view, humanism is seldom held in purist beliefs. Many humanists are not totally humanistic. The human condition, affected by depravity, dogs humanists. It prevents a whole humanism. Rejection of depravity itself leads to incomplete theory. Humanists, to work well, must believe in improvement in the nature of humankind. People must get better, not merely gain better conditions. If humans do not improve there is no permanent answer to violence, to abuse, to world problems—for the humanist. A major reason for various studies, like genetics, is to discover means for perfecting humanity.

Humanism, when present in a Christian context, is at least partly defined by the Christians through their orientation with biblical revelation. To decide that one may accept a part of the Scripture as inspired, and part not so, is to appropriate humanism to some degree. For the humanistic bent found in them, people permit themselves to become the measure of things, including revealed truth. If then they are the arbiters, their likes and dislikes, tastes and affinities are permitted to judge whether God has revealed Himself. Even if God is acknowledged, people may distort what God has said or is reputed to have said. They may deny God has revealed anything at some point, even though God has, indeed, spoken. A person's mind becomes authoritative. Variances emerge.

Even the religious person in the Christian tradition may become humanistic in belief and practice. This is dramatically illustrated by Paul C. Nagel in his *Descent from Glory*, the story of four generations of the Adams family, that included two American presidents:

> All his life, John Adams had been a deeply religious person. Until the fourth generation, most Adamses were drawn in one fashion or another to a spiritual life. Clearly both John and Abigail were sustained in their later years by faith. . . . Abigail retained from childhood a personal Christian outlook, while John's God was more general and remote.[1]

Once John was drawn into a debate with his son, John Quincy Adams, after he learned that John Quincy had endorsed the Bible and its advice to his children. John revealed his humanism, his elevation of human logic, above divine revelation:

> An incarnate God!!! An eternal, self-existent, omnipotent, omniscient author of this stupendous universe, suffering on a cross!!! My soul starts with horror at the idea, and it has stupified the Christian world. It has been the source of almost all the corruptions of Christianity.[2]

It was a developing humanism that gave the British colonies and early America the variances of Unitarianism. The biblical tradition, interpreted by the ancient Councils of the Church, cast trinitarian theology. The American controversy over the nature of God was a battle that refought the issue at Harvard College during colonial days. The cause of Unitarianism won at Harvard, but other eminent colleges supportive of trinitarianism were born out of the controversy. The conflict remains, in its manner, a controversy in our century. During the early 1980s, a flurry of debate occurred in Harvard circles when the theological school proposed that, given the growth and importance of the conservatives in the trinitarian tradition, an evangelical Christian scholar should be added to the Harvard Divinity School faculty. Spiritual immaturity sometimes reveals itself in controversies over theology in schools and denominations.

Immature Christians may accommodate the Scriptures to fit their personal determinations. In such instances, opinion about the Bible is made more important than Scripture itself. Unpopular or difficult biblical ideas are bypassed. One's own judgment is taken as sufficient for biblical interpretation. Is the opinion of this critic as good as the other? Is the judgment of a genius superior to that of a low IQ? Is rightness always on the side of the person arguing her own view most effectively?

A compelling reason why the mature Christian cannot accept humanity's equation of humanity, much less of God, is that the equation has never balanced. The evidence for humanism appears weak when all evidence is considered. People are basically good, states the humanist, because, when in proper mood, they aspire to the good. The humanist likes Anne Frank's statement that, in spite of all, man's heart is good. But aspiration is not enough to make people good. Evidence for depravity is strong, so strong that one despairs that people can survive without divine assistance. Humans cannot, unaided, solve their problems. The best they can do is postpone them. Masses of men and women demonstrate against the race to nuclear—and worse—weapons that can annihilate humankind. Leaders labor to delay that tragedy at least long enough to hand it over to future generations to manage, perhaps to delay.

The Christian's underlying premise is that people need divine assistance. People do not merit the humanist's faith placed in them to work out even their own natural salvation, to evade war and other conflicts like competitive ethnic or economic cycles. As humans we are masterful at creating our own upheavals. Most of our personal stress is self-inflicted. We are able, of course, to make some constructive choices. However, these modest achievements do not markedly strengthen the humanist's hand. Cycles upward do not get us over the top before they sag again. But we should be optimistic, the humanists say, because humanity is improving in some areas, providing confidence that more improvement will be made. Humanists reject evidence of depravity, holding to lingering faith in the ultimate perfectibility of humanity. Often humanists refer to "the dark side of man," but refuse the concept of depravity.

Mature Christians, however, carry through to the end by maintaining world- and self-views based on biblical insight. By this divine revelation they have learned how to escape from the ultimate penalty for what they are—sinners. Knowing that sin is inevitable for them—"not possible not to sin" (*non posse non pecare*), they have affirmed the Christian formula for release. They embrace all virtues related to Christ—grace, repentance, forgiveness, faith, growth and commitment. Their hope and peace generate from confidence in the truth of Scripture and its application.

A summary of the matter before us may be taken from a statement made by Malcolm Muggeridge. It is, perhaps, something of a modern summary of Solomon's perceptions in the early part of Ecclesiastes, and is Pauline in tone:

> I may, I suppose, regard myself or pass for being a relatively successful man. People occasionally stare at me in the streets—that's fame. I can fairly easily earn enough to qualify for admission to the higher slopes of the Internal Revenue—that's success. Furnished with money and a little fame even the elderly, if they care to, may partake of trendy diversions—that's pleasure. It might happen once in a while that something I said or wrote was sufficiently heeded for me to persuade myself that it represented a serious impact on our time—that's fulfillment. Yet I say to you—and I beg you to believe me—multiply these tiny triumphs by a million, add them all together, and they are nothing—less than nothing, a positive impediment—measured against one draught of that living water Christ offers to the spiritually thirsty, irrespective of who or what they are.[3]

Life's problems and issues ought to awaken for Christians a desire for clarity and knowledge about authority. The great issues are addressed clearly enough in Scripture. They should be brave, with Scripture, to take on the problems and concerns related to their commitment.

The Mature Christian Desires that Others Succeed

Mature Christians know the world is roomy enough for all its members, so they need not worry about being displaced. They are free to reach out to others. They understand that their own personal achievement usually depends upon the assistance of others, even from persons they do not know. They can acknowledge the truth of the old aphorism: "We have drunk from wells we did not dig and have been warmed at fires we did not build." Mature persons appreciate the benefits received from their ancestors and want to give back to their families and society, as well as to God, part of what was afforded to them.

Immature Christians may be ambivalent or jealous about the favorable circumstances of others. They might expect and predict failure for persons and institutions, and may nod approvingly if failure comes—believing themselves insightful. They expected failure. The failure potential for people, in some areas, is high so that prediction of failure often hits the mark. If these prophets are persons of influence, their sorrowful predictions may become self-fulfilling. They seem to have little compassion for troubled persons.

Persons educated in secular definitions of success, understanding it to be something that has highly competitive components and measurable results, may not easily understand the Christian view of success. The Christian view has its roots in God's will. Because they believe that all Christians hold a destiny in the will of God, mature persons desire to see God's will accomplished in every person. For them, understanding God's will and gaining His approval is the acme of this success. In reaching for this pinnacle they hope to gain encouragement and sustenance from others. They also provide similar support to others who seek to accomplish this mission.

Preventing high achievement is partly generated from

characteristics found in human nature: laziness, prejudice, ignorance, jealousy, greed and the like. These factors in a person or group partially block society's best purposes and plans to provide equity and opportunity for citizens. Apparently the general society is unwilling to discover how to provide equitable shares of resources for others. To the degree we are unfair, at least to that degree we are immature. Isaiah affirmed that true spirituality (even the application of fasting) is to advance freedom, to share one's bread with the hungry, to clothe and house the needy (see Isaiah 58:6-9).

The common belief is that one's success depends largely upon oneself, and while this is an important point, it is often overstated. The concept of personal responsibility was well accepted among the founders of the American nation and their descendants—at least among those commenting about it in the writings they left behind. Norman Rockwell, the artist of the middle class, was pleased that he had been taught: "The opportunity is always there. No one will prevent your success, Norman. It's up to you."

Jesus' choice of disciples suggests to us that the world does not belong only to naturally gifted men and women. His staff, composed in part of fishermen and a tax collector, made profound impact on the world. In contrast, we note that our generation boasts a person with the world's highest IQ score (officially recorded at 328, far above genius level), who is nevertheless content to produce a rather easy question and answer column for newspapers.

Despite their meager education, modest means and other limitations, the disciples were successful. And each yearned for the success of the other. They appear to have formed a brotherhood which greatly contributed to that success. Before they grew into spiritual maturity, these men were taken by competitive concepts among themselves, sometimes disappointing Jesus and each other. Some of their limitations and self dealings were moderated following Jesus' departure. The disciples found meaning for each ministry and could encourage one another even if they, being human, never lost some competitive interests.

The Mature Christian Accents Good Will

Mature Christians understand that everyone has the same perfect Creator. They also understand that depravity means that all persons share in the imperfect human condition. Accepting this given, mature Christians do not deprecate others, even though failure is the common experience for all. Mature persons simply refuse to think ill of neighbors and fellow Christians. John Donne, the poetic Christian divine, reminded his readers that they could not diminish others without diminishing themselves.

Mature Christians, then, will affirm the better side, and avoid emphasizing the darker. Focusing on the better side, they know they will more likely become problem solvers than problem reactors. Admittedly this is difficult to do in a society influenced by media forms obsessed with the gossip, the foibles, the failures, the sins of others. Knowing that persons fail, the mature are not alarmed and learn how to grant benefit of doubt in human behavior. They utilize expectations for improvement. Their designs and strategies draw upon possibilities. There is magnetism—sometimes weak, sometimes strong—but magnetism nonetheless between expectation and realization.

Immature men and women divide the population into good and evil, based on their own views of good and evil, especially in politics. Persons in authority are generally on the wrong side of issues. Most actions are to be treated with skepticism. No one practices integrity: motives are to be doubted. So follows the litany generated by doubt, fear and suspicion.

Mature persons desire to grant anyone the benefit of the doubt about human conduct. Where there is doubt there must be, at the least, delay in judgment. Patience increases with practice. Mature persons require evidence before they believe accusations against others. They force themselves to wait for it. Patience in practice is prayer that God will accomplish His will on His schedule.

Mature Christians learn to be kind. Biblical kindness teaches balance between firmness and sensitivity. That sensitivity is primarily awareness about attitudes and conducts related to the effective advancement of the gospel. Kindness may ready persons to be receptive to the message of God. It is a grace that may create spiritual acceptance in others. It is not a sensitivity that protects the Christian from being hurt by others.

The Mature Christian
Knows that Models Fail

Mature Christians do not falsify heroes. They know that a person may be a genius and a cad, an effective leader and a personal failure. King David becomes a prime illustration of the paradoxes of eminent persons. Even Christian heroes, like the apostle Paul, or Augustine or Martin Luther, were flawed in this or that feature of their lives. We like near perfection in our life models, but we ought to know that, with the exception of Jesus, we will never find it. Mature persons manage contradictions, even those found in their models.

Immature persons may put too great confidence in heroes, especially those they believe are eminent. So they commonly believe their models are to be emulated by all persons. When the intimate truth of one or more of their heroes is published, the immature may flag in faith and conduct. They lack resources to deal with this kind of disappointment. Out of such occasions they may miss the fact that ideals remain even when they are not practiced. Beethoven's symphonies cannot be judged by the way the local high school band plays them. Baseball is a better game than I played it. Christ and His message cannot be faulted because uncertain and casual persons, playing at religion, represent it poorly.

When their hero's ideas are found to be weak, immature people may be weakened in faith. When the model fails, they permit that failure to open the door for their own personal failure. They find it difficult to get around their support patterns for survival. They, the weak, tend to relate to celebrities (such as media personalities) more than heroes. They are not discreet in choices. They likely do not know the celebrities they idolize. Even so, personality cultism grows for them, and they like the way they "feel." Referring to First Corinthians 3:21-23, Wendell Grout, a long-time and insightful minister, rightly pointed out three marks of immaturity: 1) following personalities rather than valuing the contributions that all Christians can make, 2) equating blessing with personal excitement and/or success, and 3) occupying oneself with a quest for security rather than resting in commitment to Jesus Christ. Each of these three concepts identifies some of the characteristics of immature Christians, and two (1 and 3), add characteristics of maturity.

Immature Christians tend to contrast the well-known person (a major hero for them) to a local minister (a minor or sub-hero for them) to the disadvantage of the local. Many a minister, with miniscule budget, overburdened schedule and limited authority is put down in a conflict created by the followers of the impressive, widely funded, remote, sometimes charismatic celebrity of radio and television ministries. The comparison is entirely inappropriate. Circumstances are not comparable. But the contrasts are permitted to prevail for the immature person.

We may not qualify as sound analysts of ourselves or our situations. A man at a conference center came for counsel. He found himself angered often. He became angry with people with whom he felt disagreement. He would even get angry with people who were not in agreement with people he liked, especially his favorite media ministers. He sent his tithes and offerings to several radio personalities and gave almost nothing to his local church. The errors he found in the church leaders and members were the errors of many, even most, persons, including himself. Ultimately, his harsh attitudes and words were directed toward discrediting the church. By his actions, with several acquaintances assisting him, his predictions became self-fulfilling in that church. He was immature.

The man believed readily the disappointing evidence about his local church situation. But he held a gracious opinion about the distant media personality. Several of the media persons he supported were much less than he believed them to be. Deploring divorce by a local minister, he nevertheless supported a thrice divorced radio evangelist. And he knew the circumstances. He applied two standards. Some of his giving indicated poor stewardship. Even so, several of the media ministers he supported were excellent.

Heroes have feet of clay. Knowing their friends and colleagues can fail, mature people themselves can function in at least two important ways: 1) avoid becoming the cause for unsatisfactory conduct in other persons, which is to avoid becoming a cause of temptation; and 2) provide modeling influence and counsel, demonstrating the benefits of maturity. A mature person may even make up for weakness in an immature. This has often occurred in a marriage in which one mate (like an Abigail) overcomes the failure of the other (like a Nabal). Abigail is a biblical model of maturity.

A mature Christian may inspire non-Christians to make better decisions for themselves and their institutions. Crossover influences go both ways in the social and political world. Anyone knowing the inner workings of government and other vital institutions, has seen the process at work—Christians and non-Christians working together to achieve personal and social improvement. The mature Christian, even at his or her best, is imperfect, and can permit imperfection in others. This acceptance does not condone poor conduct, but recognizes its inevitability and adjusts to it.

The Mature Christian
Finds Balance in God's Creation

Mature Christians respect nature. These persons consciously live in the environment of nature and protect it while using it. Their relationships with nature provide information useful for excellence in stewardship and responsibility. Their awe of creation coincides with the biblical affirmation of nature where creation is God's doing and the heavens reflect His glory. Much of what God commands of the race relates to humanity's adjustment to nature. This is noted, for example, in the biblical cleanliness laws and in the need for alternate work and rest, as taught in the Pentateuch. A linkage is made between God in nature and God in social history. God's laws are not arbitrary.

Immature persons may distort creation. They defy it, run against it, trash it. When they do, health and well-being can be and often are negatively affected. Their habits tell on them and debilitate them. They cannot fight nature and maintain themselves well. Nor can they inflate the meaning of nature as it relates to humanity without distorting it. They may interpret nature as a kind of god, and themselves as chiefs among many animals in the god-invested environment. They may become pantheistic. This viewpoint distorts their understanding of nature's proper use. For them any pollution at all may be evil. They seem not to admit that some pollution is unavoidable, and that nature can manage minor violations. The mature person has a balanced sense of nature—both of its power and its fragility.

But immature Christians are often unwilling to understand and accept this balance. Some, taking on anti-intellectual attitudes, do not even try to work out the equation. They build their views on emotions, their own subjective feelings. Evidence and logic mean little to them, and they are suspicious of intellectual persons, even before they have heard available ideas and evidence.

Humanists are understandably suspicious, even disdainful, of these immature persons. Much of the humanist criticism of Christianity is based on caricatures of the immature, anti-intellectual Christian. Unhappily for the Church, some immature Christians receive media coverage, creating, for the general public, an illusion of credence for the skeptic's critique.

During the early 1980s, for example, a religious television celebrity succeeded in persuading his followers to resist any social plan of population control. Among his specious arguments was the claim that "all the population of the world can be accommodated in Texas in single family homes." If there were no other social consideration than square footage of land per person, nothing more need be said—Texas could indeed hold the world's population. But the statement addressed none of the large related issues: quality of life; availability and quantities of resources; purity of water, air and soils; dispersal of waste products; costs of services, fuels and the like. His statement loomed up from ignorance and arrogance.

Mature Christians do not buy into such naive thinking. They are friends of science in factual areas, even if not in some of the theories. Where thinking humanists differ from thinking Christians is primarily in the area of the authority of biblical faith, and the resulting, conflicting interpretations of available facts in nature. The intellectual humanist or agnostic views creation as origin whereas the Christian sees it as a result. The humanist proposes that creation caused its own beginning in an evolutionary or other process unassisted by intelligence. Christians, on the other hand, see the creation as a result of God's working intelligently in eternity.

The mature Christian focuses on the Creator. He or she believes that the Creator was at the beginning and all else that followed was merely a result of His design—including the creation of the universe. The Christian is not so concerned with exactly how and when the Creator did what He did, but rather for what purpose He did it and what will be the conclusion of the matter. Endings are intellectually and practically more important than beginnings for believers. The Christian relies on Scripture to discover whatever specific information is available from God, especially about endings.

But the humanist wishes to discover what happened at the beginning of nature and thereafter, how it happened and at what time. He looks to the "developing cosmos" to find out. His great omission is to disregard the Author who understands what He did, and who reveals a part, a small part, of the story (see Deuteronomy 29:29).

In general, humanists admire the creation and hope God is not introduced to muddy the picture. For them, something is deeply wrong if God does exist. They wonder, for example, why there is famine. Like persons who fail to integrate their lives in a healthy, holistic way, humanists usually cannot integrate the acts of nature into one panoramic picture. They may diminish one act of God by overemphasizing another. An earthquake or typhoon is an act of God, but so is the birth of a baby. A flood is an act of God. So is an abundant harvest. In fact, harvests and floods are often closely related.

We return to wholeness again, not only in ourselves, but in the creation. The winds of one hemisphere blow over another, for good or ill. The pollution of a state registers itself in snows at the poles. The acid rain of one nation falls on another. There is no escape—what occurs in the part occurs in the whole. What is done in one place has meaning for all places.

The "butterfly effect" is believed by some theorists. The theory holds that if we had instruments sensitive enough, and we were placed on a distant planet in the solar system, we could measure the effect upon that planet of the flutter of the wings of a single butterfly on earth. If there is such an effect, we will be even more impressed about the larger influence each person makes upon creation.

So then, are famine, pestilence and acts of God evidence of an unloving, uncaring Creator? Or are they more often the results of people's folly, in the uses and misuses of the earth and its resources? Mature Christians understand that nature is the close friend of humankind, if humankind will be its friend. They see that even natural disasters can serve the race, if people will permit God, who oversees His creation, to direct their attention and conduct.

The Mature Christian Possesses a Sense of Humor

The mature Christian does not take the personal self too seriously. These persons know that they will sometimes miss the mark, that others see things differently than they do, and that humor is healing and prophetic in its way. No matter how incongruous a situation may be, humor implies questions. Humor suggests a look at life from an elevated vantage point. The situations for humor are as many as one can find. Even persons who outlived death in concentration camps stated they were carried along by humor to survival. Humorless victims died. Henry Ware wrote: "A good jest in time of misfortune is food and drink."

It is interesting that totalitarian societies are humorless in their public presentation of their governments and leaders. If genuine humor could be developed between heads of state, would the military threat of nations be so great? Not likely. Those heads would more likely see themselves entering the stage, strutting through the act, and exiting on the other side, as fresh actors enter to take their parts. During the thaw between Russia and the United States in the late 1980s, humor, even repartee, emerged between leaders. Mainland China held rigid during the period, remaining humorless in exchange between leaders.

Immature persons may fear that humor will find them out. They protect themselves. They may reveal their immaturity in unnecessary defensiveness. They cannot bear any accent of themselves that is not laudatory or complimentary. If it is not favorable, then silence is preferred. Solemnity takes over. They are often embarrassed in interpersonal situations, fearing they will become the butt of a joke. They react to the inner fear of making a public "scene" of any kind, no matter how innocent and human. Almost anything happening to them in relationship with others is interpreted as a put-down. These men and women are not easy to talk to, and they seem judgmental. A casual remark may be turned into a distortion, either inwardly for themselves, or outwardly involving others. They become dour. Life loses flavor. Humor is a condiment for an otherwise bland life. Even so these people may secretly wish they could enjoy life as others seem to do, especially those others who have come to terms with themselves.

Am I the last one to know who I am, or how I am perceived? Humor has in it some of the information I need about myself, even about my faith. I can know something of myself and what is happening to me, I am told, in my tears (and what motivates them), but also in my laughter (and what motivates it). (See Ecclesiastes 3:1-4.)

Humor suggests hope when problems are severe, and it intimates humility—sometimes homely humility—when all seems well. There is a give-and-take, a repartee, a kind of genuine foolishness that relates to others and ourselves. Humor is integral to the wholeness that characterizes mature Christians. There is balance in humor when humor is genuine. Observers of business meetings have seen chairpersons use humor to defuse tense debate, even restore friendships. By that technique verbal gladiators are brought back to gentility, reality and balance. When we find humorless persons we feel something important is missing in them.

The underlying premise here is that humor helps set us

free. The concept is major in William F. May's *A Catalogue of Sins*, in which the author makes reference to humor and the "surplus of grace." Whatever the nature and extent of sin, there is an abundance of divine grace that overpowers sin. This delights us—or ought to. We rightly turn to comedy then as one way to express our ultimate freedom and victory. May argues that this excess of grace has been more effectively treated in comedy than in systematic theology.

What a gift is humor! As already noted elsewhere, humor, practiced sensibly, has provided healing for the sick, has made concentration camps bearable, has maintained difficult daily human exchanges, and has stimulated energy for future assignments. It has provided entry to recovery from failure, and has broken down barriers to relationships. It has provided a route of return from weariness, suspicion, even fallacious thinking.

Humor can point the emotions to better directions than they may otherwise take. The eminent preacher, Charles Spurgeon, was partly eminent because of his humor. Without humor, Abraham Lincoln believed he would die under the burden of his office. If we believe Elton Trueblood, Jesus had an effective sense of humor. His story of the beam and speck in an eye brought laughter, we may be sure—given the standards of Jewish imagination and humor in the first century of our era.

The Mature Christian Responds Constructively to His Own Weaknesses

Mature Christians do not rationalize personal weaknesses. They know their own weaknesses, and also know that all human beings have weaknesses. They gain confidence in discovering their weaknesses and seeking to improve themselves. For example, an administrator who manages detail work poorly, and admits that he does, is a candidate for improving himself in that regard. In acknowledging that he is unsatisfactory in his performance, the administrator may solicit assistance from others. He may even ask them to cover in acceptable ways for him. Many effective ministers, knowing their strengths and weaknesses, have related to colleagues in such a manner that not only are their weaknesses met by talented others, but those ministers have larger blocks of time to do what they do well. These realistic persons, if they are respectful of the work of others, become excellent team workers. If all members have similar weaknesses, that team may expect problems that frustrate their purposes.

Immature persons commonly hold strong urges to rationalize their weaknesses. They feel they cannot afford to fail or take blame in any way. So they make excuses to distract even themselves from making adjustments. Many of their excuses (e.g., "everybody is trying to get us") are familiar. They are repeated so often that perceptive listeners disregard them on reflection. Persons who work with immature colleagues must learn how to avoid being thwarted in projects. Even so, some delays are likely.

Generally, issues of interest to immature persons are not as important as implied or argued. They are not usually destructive to well-ordered projects. If we have a choice and issues are important, we work around wounded or easily wounded persons for solving problems. If we cannot, projects flounder. In such cases, mature persons generally bow quietly out of the group.

The immature person tends to blame teachers, parents, mates and others for what he or she feels is failure or omission in his or her experience. Psychologists assert that blaming and shaming others is a significant sign of immaturity. They treat clients for the problem. Counselors hear a lot of "blame" talk from clients. They may need to redirect the conversation. Can this client make any corrective gesture? Will he or she become something of a problem solver rather than an aggravator of problems?

Daniel Goleman asked a common question, "What really makes people satisfied with their lives?" The answer was open but clear: "The secret may lie in a person's ability to

handle life's blows without passivity, blame or bitterness."
Goleman referred to a study of 173 Harvard graduates from
the early 1940s. If the men, at 65 years of age, were perceived to be emotionally healthy, they would have a clear
ability to play, to work, to love and to feel satisfaction with
life.[4]

The men were contacted from time to time for the nearly
50 years following their commencements, with results reported in the *American Journal of Psychiatry.* The men who
fared well in the study were practical, dependable, and
close to their children at college age. They were not significantly affected by their own childhood problems, even
those perceived generally as devastating. Several did suffer
depression at some point along the years, usually caused by
persistent emotional or physical problems. But they were
adaptable to life. They found a potent predictor of well-being was the ability to treat emotional crisis naturally, by
controlling the first impulse in the rising crisis, and by giving measured response to it. The mature person met a
problem head-on as soon as he recognized it.

Mature Christians are through with making scapegoats.
By taking responsibility for themselves, they are able to
move past their weaknesses and on to sensible solutions.
They clear the table and make ready for the next course.
Christianity emphasizes this matter of self-responsibility.
The theology of redemption stresses that every person
must make his or her own decision for or against his or her
own salvation (Ezekiel 18). To respond favorably to the call
for my own salvation is a vital step toward managing weaknesses. Regarding duty, we are commanded to "work out
[our] salvation with fear and trembling" (Philippians 2:12).

The Mature Christian
Determines to Act Responsibly

Mature Christians do what they ought to do. Studies
show that we, as individuals, generally believe we are giv-

ing more than our share, more than others are giving. When the facts are known, seldom can it be shown that we are doing more for good or benefit than we ought to do. Rather, mature people usually feel they might reasonably do more than they are doing to meet human needs. They do not measure performance by comparison with others, but by the needs of people and their own resources. Jesus informed Peter not to judge his own performance by John's, nor John's by his.

Immature persons may feel unable to cope with life's duties. An immature man or woman often feels unable, or unwilling, to meet even standard expectations. There is a constant feeling that life is unfair, too much intrusion on personal time and resources is taking place, too much is being asked or expected, even tacitly. These persons suspect they are "burning out." So their need for distraction or rest and recreation increases. They require more and more time for escape and recuperation.

Immature persons always have excuses why something cannot be done about world, family, economic or other problems. They commonly resist, perhaps in subdued ways, leaders they could depend upon to guide them through to solutions. They protest that the project will cost too much, or that no one knows where it will finally end, or that there will not be enough time to complete it. And while these objections may be valid on occasion, often they are not.

It is important to recognize that most of the things we ought to do we can indeed do. If we cannot do something, even with the help of others, then we need not be unduly troubled about either the project or our inability to accomplish it. Evidence shows that many men and women become stressful about matters over which they have no control.

But the reverse is our major concern here. Everyone who is able to accomplish a good, even create an opportunity to do so, ought to be active about that business. They rightly feel twinges of guilt if they evade servant roles. Everyone faces a lifetime of judgments about what he or she can and cannot do. A mature person sifts those judgments.

It is essential in making these judgments to acknowledge the sovereignty of God. He will not expect from anyone more than that person can do, but He does expect all to carry out the tasks He assigns. Ministers are to act as ministers ought to act. Mothers and fathers should effectively perform their roles. Presidents, farmers, kings and taxicab drivers can, in confidence of God's provision, accomplish their assignments.

Mature Christians are not daunted by their tasks, even when extenuating circumstances arise, because they understand that whatever happens—even illness, poverty or war—is to be interpreted through the sovereignty of God. Why should world problems diminish a Christian's faith? Or why should they take away his duty? The mature Christian accepts his or her own responsibility and willingly performs it, in pleasant circumstances or ill, under the provision of God.

The Mature Christian Rejects Exploitation

Mature Christians do not use persons without their permission. These persons know that much of the world's evil demonstrates itself through personal exploitation. Slaves have been exploited by slaveholders. Soldiers have been exploited by warmongers. Peasants have been exploited by landholders. Industrialists have exploited laborers; laborers have exploited industrialists. The long story, often sordid and/or violent, has been recited many times. These are litanies that disgrace us as the human race. Claiming human rights for ourselves, we ought not deny equality to others by exploiting them. Slavery, prostitution and various other similar societal and human sins are objectionable partly because they are highly exploitive.

Immature persons tend to seek their own ends without

sufficient concern about personal costs to others. They may disregard the principles of responsible self-determination for each man and woman. They tend to seek their own ends without concern about personal costs to others. This is found in their exploitation of their parents, perhaps of their mates and families, or others. They interpret their own actions as ethical so that exploiting others expands their own conjured virtues.

But all people are temporarily, for their lifetimes, their own moral agents—for good or ill. No one except God has the right to interfere with or block the practice of an individual in the exercise of that agency, except to the degree it impinges upon the rights of others. Presumably, both enlightened conscience and democratic laws inform persons about the social/personal rights of citizens. The mature Christian wishes to be democratic. Even freedom has its limits.

A sense of personal worth should characterize each person. We tend to evaluate ourselves by externals—by the amount of money we make, by the family we were born into or created, by the power we wield, by the approvals from others we gain. But sense of worth ought to stem from the opinion God holds of us. God is knowledgeable about each person, even, as the Gospels state, to the count of the hairs of his or her head. The worth of each person, we learn, is greater than the world's worth. Our worth is partly seen in that we are called to do God's service. As far as we know only angels and humankind are included in that special calling. Nature's formula seems straightforward. Animals serve humans, but humans serve God—or ought to. Just as animals are free, but domesticated to humans, so humans are free but domesticated to God.

Recognition of human worth should demonstrate itself in compassion for people—by people as well as God. It is easier to accept ourselves and others when we believe that God regards us as objects worth His special attention. Rather than judge people for their weaknesses, we regard them for both their best human and spiritual potential.

Proper recognition of worth respects the rights of others: their rights to their own status, to their own time, and to their own reputations. When it is at full power, recognition allows for human differences, even peculiarities. It does not force the meaning of "normal." What is normal among people and nations? We do not know. There is little that may be characterized as normal.

Exploitation can be avoided through team relationships freely engaged. In this way equals work together. There is a job to be done, and it cannot be done without team effort. The free spirit leaves it to the individual to identify with, or turn away from, opportunity. Perhaps fewer persons will participate than a draft would enlist, but those who do participate by their own choice express their own maturity. Rebellion and bitterness are consequences of compulsory sacrifice, even when beneficial human service is performed.

There are those who may share our vision. They give to it, even sacrifice for it. They could not accomplish that vision alone, or even enjoy it. They would not have known what to do with it without fellow volunteers to achieve it. Significant missions in the kingdom of God have been accomplished by a group effort in which team members believed and acted together. It then becomes a corporate vision to which the members volunteer themselves.

There are many who identify with our mission. In a sense it becomes their mission. Out of the vision comes mission—or is it the other way around? We are not concerned about which is first. One does not have significant meaning without the other. Neither will likely make much difference without sufficient resources and people engaged with corporate effort. Creativity is larger for a team when the matter at hand relates to a corporate vision. We rightly encourage individuals with their own personal vision and creativity. But mature Christians know that important visions usually require teamwork to become reality. Lone Ranger work is limited. Even the Ranger had his native friend to assist him.

A family, corporation or church is a team—or ought to be—calling on its members to give of themselves in ways that fulfill roles and accomplish worthy goals. The basic team in society is represented in the family. Other corporate teams relate primordially to that team. But each team member needs to find his own balance between appropriate group involvement and self-sacrifice. No one other than the individual or God possesses independent authority to sacrifice his or her time or resources. Without such freedom, balance in a free society, in families, in businesses, even in churches will not occur.

The Mature Christian Learns Self-Control

Mature Christians resist the urge to respond only on emotional bases. No matter what other people may say or do, mature people practice self-control, bearing up even under verbal attacks or in controversial exchanges. They listen and prepare responses, rejecting natural urges to answer in negative ways. They can afford to permit others to say whatever they want to say.

Immature persons may respond negatively in their emotions, especially if they feel threatened. They may say or do things they regret later—or ought to. They may stick to their reactions because they have affirmed positions and cannot comfortably retreat. They sometimes win the argument, even when they are wrong, and some venture will be diminished, delayed, even lost because they prevailed. Those experienced in church ministries know about congregations lost to their parent bodies, or split into separate groups, or even dissolved because fiery but immature members prevailed in a conflict.

Mature people try to avoid physical or verbal responses that cause loss of self-control in themselves or others. They learn, "a soft answer turneth away wrath" (Proverbs 15:1, KJV). A "soft answer" is evidence of self-control. Soft is not that the argument is weak or diluted. It is controlled. Self-control is seldom acceptable counsel for the hotheaded, but it is respectful and friendly to both truth and feelings. Objective reply, well spoken, is given in the hope of solving problems, not for the purpose of emotional responses.

Mature men and women understand the value of exercising self-control under trying circumstances because they know that God sometimes uses opposition to instruct them. They recognize that what is beneficial in their lives does not always feel good. They understand that useful results can accrue even from negative, unjustified opposition.

Joseph told his brothers that when they sold him into slavery in Egypt they meant it for ill, but that God meant it for good. Because he had this divine perception, Joseph was able to refrain from reacting emotionally to his negative and unfair circumstances. He understood that problems caused by natural ill winds, blowing out of everyday circumstances, can nevertheless be applied constructively.

Some leaders in current society also recognize the value of maintaining self-control under difficult circumstances, understanding that such circumstances often represent irreplaceable opportunity. Jesse Jackson, African-American sometime aspirant for nomination to the American presidency, made the point repeatedly. He said that the poor have an experience that leads them to virtue, an experience the rich do not have. His theory suggests that because black people are, on the average, poorer than whites, they may be "superior" in some ways because they have a wider range of experience.

Jackson argued that he was equally at home with the rich and the poor since he lived among both groups. He was born in humble circumstances to a young unwed black girl, but later became affluent. Jackson contended that his upper-crust peer group did not have the same advantage since they, whether black or white, were born into and maintained wealth. He believed their wealth kept them from moving easily among different segments of the population. Political reporter Walt Harrington summarized Jackson's views in an article that appeared in *Washington Post Magazine:*

> Jesse Jackson says a lot of things you can't take at face value, so many balls does he keep in the air. But one thing he says so many times, so many ways that I believe he believes it, plain and simple: Life at the bottom is a fuller, richer life than life at the top. Here is where race and class finally meet in Jackson's mind. He says poor people—from before the time of Christ, black or white—have always been the voice of conscience. Their vantage is superior. It's why the Christmas angel visited shepherds, not kings. It is the rich who lack insight. It's their deficit, their problem. It was their problem when Jackson was a boy; it is their problem today. As he said, "The privileged haven't any story."[5]

Although Jackson did not account for the affluent Magi—also summoned to worship the Child—the point made was that experience, even if at first presumed negative, can later on serve for good. The deciding factor is how those facing difficult experiences will use them—will they exercise self-control and a humble patience? Or will they waste the opportunity?

Much may be learned about ourselves by analyzing what people do who engage in dramatic or creative, even dangerous, work. Note how men and women talk and act who solve great problems, lead dynamic companies, even those who defuse bombs or put out raging fires. They seem to be special persons. Is there inherent wisdom in them? In a Montana forest fire, untrained men broke and ran against the advice of an old-timer working a hill with them. They died on the ridge of the hill. The man later said the youths died because they were inexperienced and would not stand ground with him. His colleagues agreed with him. It was another way of saying the young men were immature.

The Mature Christian Seeks Understanding

Mature Christians do not skirt truth and its real meaning. These persons prefer reality and find it easier than alternatives to deal with, even when it seems threatening to them. They dismiss lies or rosy fantasies. Mature people may dislike what they learn to be the actual situation. They prepare themselves to treat matters realistically. Mature persons know that matters may not be as they appear.

Immature persons accept what seems obvious to them. They often act upon what they wish to be true. They do not bother finding truth if truth seems, in their modest reflection, to be too demanding. If they did find it, they might have to invest themselves more than they wish in order to gain balance and solve problems. Finding and acting on truth requires directed energy, and such energy is generally in low supply in immature persons.

An underlying premise here is that real life issues can be understood by persons holding biblical faith. The open secret is to investigate facts or alleged facts until each matter is clear, and the investigator is confident of the case. This became a compelling process for me while speaking during a week at a conference. The ministry, although satisfactory, was not as effective as I expected it to be. Everyone was gracious to me, and attentive, but something seemed "wrong." Down deep I sensed a problem. Soon it became clear that there was a pervasive habit of gossip common to many of the men and women in attendance. Someone would start a story in the morning; by nightfall it had spread throughout the conference. I became intrigued. Nothing quite like it had ever occurred in my experience. I decided to follow up several stories I heard, and talk about them in the light of biblical teaching.

Story #1: "The bookstore at the conference is making big

profits so the campers can expect a decline in future conference charges."

Fact: The husband and wife team was asked to bring an inventory of books and to dedicate their time to sales and to the making of recordings of the guest speakers. They were instructed to keep the money they earned from the books—a modest, normal week's income similar to what the couple received when they worked in their own store. Profit from the speaker tapes, a few hundred dollars, went to the conference for extra expenses. There was no truth in the campers' gossipy story.

Story #2: "The Christian college in a large city nearby is out of funds and about to close. There is no use sending money for its support."

Fact: Not only was the school not closing, but it had just received a government grant of $150,000, with more to follow, that would assist its growth. Although the college still needed support, it continues to flourish. There was no truth in story #2.

Story #3: "The camp manager is harried and badly treated by his board because, among all his other duties, he must pump the septic tank daily."

Fact: For the busiest weeks during the summer the tank might need to be pumped three times a week. It had never been pumped as often as two days in a row. The manager usually did not do the pumping; when he did, he chose entirely on his own to do it, and he found no objection in doing so. Ordinarily an outside company would come in to do the job for a modest fee. There was no truth in story #3.

When individuals do not seek truth and understanding, they create negative impressions of themselves and others. They can impede effective ministry, as these campers did. If they had been more mature, they would have wished to know the truth so that they could make rational judgments.

In their quest for understanding and truth, mature people ask a lot of questions: What is really going on here?

Who has the answers? What are those answers? How do we manage this information? But despite all their questions, mature people also realize that they will not find answers to everything. They know that understanding includes accepting their ignorance as well as their knowledge. When understanding gains balance between what is known and what is unknown, it commends the holders, and gives them help in problem-solving.

Mature Christians are characterized by right thinking, right attitudes, right action. They learn to settle their own personal issues and to reach beyond themselves to help others. They nurture constructive relationships with others. They actively, sometimes unflaggingly, work to develop their character, employing objective standards by which to evaluate that character. They are always seeking truth and are fulfilled when they find it. Mature Christians learn to live effectively, enjoying the journey and anticipating the destination.

The Mature Christian . . .

- lives a life of wholeness
- follows the biblical compass
- desires others to succeed
- accents good will in others
- knows that models fail
- finds balance in creation
- possesses a sense of humor
- responds constructively to personal weaknesses
- determines to act responsibly
- rejects exploitation of other persons
- learns self-control
- seeks enlightened understanding

Endnotes

1 Nagel, Paul C. *Descent from Glory* (New York: Oxford University Press, 1983), p. 128.

2 Ibid. (original source: Adams Papers in the archives of the Massachusetts Historical Society).

3 Porter, David. *The Practical Christianity of Malcolm Muggeridge* (Downers Grove, IL: InterVarsity Press, 1983). Copyright by David Porter, p. 5.

4 Goleman, Daniel. "Secret to Happiness," *Reader's Digest,* October 1990, p. 16 (summarized from *The New York Times*).

5 Harrington, Walt. "On the Road with the President of Black America," *Washington Post Magazine,* January 25, 1987, p. 45.

_____ *Chapter*
_____ *5*

The Pattern of Christian Values

But the wisdom that is from above is first pure, then peaceable, gentle, and easy to be entreated, full of mercy and good fruits, without partiality, and without hypocrisy. (James 3:17, KJV)

Spiritual wisdom—identified as wisdom "from above" by the apostle James—provides perceptions for a mature Christian philosophy and lifestyle. This divine wisdom is revealed, whereas human wisdom arises from serious reflection about human experience. In the revealed wisdom, according to James, there is virtue, peace, gentleness, openness, mercy, acceptance, integrity and good works. No other biblical declaration quite parallels this remarkable single-verse summary.

James offered this succinct definition with the implication, in the whole of the epistle, that wisdom, whether from above or from reflective experience, relates to maturity. The emphasis here is on God's viewpoint. The integrated person gaining divine wisdom will develop a conduct pattern characterized by spiritual, personal and psychological maturity. In summary, there is human wisdom, practical for the life of a person and secular society, and spiritual wisdom practical for persons preparing for immortality. When understood and practiced rightly they are not in conflict.

The Christian Should Be Pure, Therefore Peaceable

Few men and women connect the ideas and functions of peace and purity. The Bible offers a number of biographical sketches of persons who failed to make the connection, or to make it and hold on to the end. A notable example is King David. When David expressed his desire to build a temple for the Lord, he was denied because, as a warrior, he had shed blood (see 1 Chronicles 28:3). David had been a remarkable soldier, and became an effective king, humanly wise in the matters of statehood: "So he shepherded them according to the integrity of his heart, and guided them by the skillfulness of his hands" (Psalm 78:72, NKJV). As a soldier, David was contrasted to King Saul, also an honored soldier, as 10 times more effective. By Old Testament reports, succeeding on the battlefield was believed to be divine blessing, in the assumption that the dead were God's enemies.

God's standard is reverence for life, not only as explicitly taught in Scripture, but implied in nature and in general biblical concepts, like laws for cleansing after a person had touched a dead body. Not until a person, even burying a deceased family member, was cleansed, could he return to worship among the people (see Numbers 19). Sanctity for life is a concept carrying promises of blessing to those who honor it (see Deuteronomy 22:6-7). In this passage from Deuteronomy, the same promise is given for the care of animal life as that for honoring one's parents—long life on earth. In light of this value for life, King David was denied his great objective because of his prowess in killing, even killing the enemies of God's people. Although disappointed, David appears to have understood the principle.

God's house, as the Tenant would have it, must be built by a man of peace. Meeting the peace prerequisite, David's son, Solomon, whose name means peace, was permitted to direct the construction of the temple. Solomon became, even in secular culture, synonymous with "wisdom" and his writings are known as wisdom literature. As the years elapsed, Solomon appears to have possessed wisdom (secular) as a ruler of a state without fully applying revealed wisdom (spiritual) in his personal life. His many marriages interlocked his nation with surrounding kingdoms for peace (secular wisdom), but mingling the religions of his wives with his own caused dilution of the faith revealed through Moses (spiritual wisdom). That spelled catastrophe for the purposes of Israel. God would have provided peace without violation of revelation, the Word that is eternally true. Continuing violation of spiritual wisdom was cause for a litany of stories about succeeding kings who sinned and failed. The paradox of excellence in some features, and naivete in others, as seen in David and Solomon, is common in men and women in any era.

Centuries later, Jesus rejected violation of the purity and peace principle. In His model of peace, Jesus revealed purity. He became, He becomes, a purveyor of peace and purity. One may lead to the other, but the accent here is on purity that leads to peace for the individual or the group. Not all lovers of peace love purity. They fervently desire peace, but are unwilling to invest themselves for it. The failure to relate sufficiently well peace with purity may account for the inability of followers of persons like Mohandas Gandhi and Martin Luther King to gain goals of passive resistance. Responses of many, affirming to be their followers, have been violent. Maturity relates to the practice of purity to peace.

Although purity is related to peace, it is also related to power. Wherever there is a share of purity, there is a share of power. The greater the Christian's purity, the greater intrinsic power. Power is different than force, and Jesus held power. His power was illustrated in the reaction of the centurion at the point of deep darkness: "Surely he was the Son of God!" (Matthew 27:54), and in the repentance of one of the robbers who hung beside Jesus: "We are punished justly, for we are getting what our deeds deserve. But this man has done nothing wrong. . . . Jesus, remember me when you come into your kingdom" (Luke 23:41-42). Even inanimate objects responded to His power in the splitting of the temple veil. The force of Roman might is now a story of ancient decline, faded glory from among nations. Christ remains in power, named the primary influence of history. From His followers, sons and daughters are named, and in His name they pray.

The Christian Should Be Gentle, Therefore Open to Entreaty

The mature person is gentle and responsive to others, reflecting Christlikeness. God's character, revealed in His Son, Jesus, became gentleness personified. God is responsive to entreaty, as evidenced by His readiness to hear and answer prayers. In turn, ready response to genuine human entreaty (like unto prayer) characterizes mature Christians.

Wisdom that comes from God, as James affirmed, is gentle, resulting in useful knowledge and gentle persuasion. Jesus offers an example of the exercise of these qualities. Although the disciples tried to block children from Jesus, Jesus would not permit it. "Let the little children come to me," He said (Mark 10:14). Jesus welcomed the mothers' entreaty and the responses of the children, suggesting that adults should follow the meek example found in the children. The number of occasions is large that Jesus responded to entreaty, sometimes focusing the attitude, as a part of His instruction to His disciples to act compassionately.

A practical illustration of entreaty appears out of the lives of a trio in the early Church. Apollos—fervent, articulate and knowledgeable in the Scripture—preached the baptism of repentance taught by John the Baptist. He had not yet heard the message of Christ. Aquila and Priscilla diplomatically presented the full gospel story. Apollos was persuaded, partly through their gentleness and wisdom. Apollos, open to entreaty, gave them a hearing. Actual events may have taken days or weeks. Aquila and Priscilla, perhaps not so talented nor holding so high status as Apollos, made entreaty for Christ. Apollos received the message, converted, and became a gifted preacher in the early Church (see Acts 18:18-28).

Apollos also fulfilled mature attitudes in the discussion, listening to persons who were lesser in ability and public acclaim than he. If wisdom makes gentleness, and gentleness causes appropriate responsiveness, we find them in order and effective with these three persons. Gospel information was served up in an attractive manner. Apollos became a Christian.

Gentleness is sometimes related to power and strength, as can readily be illustrated in nature. Animals of great physical strength—elephants, leopards, lions—care gently for their offspring. In the presence of danger, several large elephants will surround an elephant calf for protection. He is surrounded by huge bodies, but is untouched by any and will not be. They face outward in every direction, standing so near one another that nothing can penetrate to the center where the calf stands. If the adults were to move too far inward, the calf would be crushed, but this will not happen. The strength of the elephants is more admired because it is controlled by gentleness. There is nothing to fear in the elephants' strength unless it is challenged.

Strong men and women must decide how they will use their strength. If so inclined they can crush things and injure people. Not all strength is physical. Arrogance in the strong is manifestation of pride, opposed to gentleness. It therefore prevents entreaty. Arrogant people are closed to persuasion. Insensitive to others, they refuse fairness. Competing ideas to their own are downgraded. First in their own estimation, correct in all their opinions, they have nothing to learn. Their self-centeredness remains to motivate their conduct. Their strength does not lead to gentleness, therefore is unrelated to maturity.

The Christian Should Be Full of Mercy, Therefore Full of Good Fruits

Jesus was moved deeply by the listening crowd and, after a lengthy period, broke off ministry to provide merciful rest for exhausted disciples, only by the same mercy to be drawn back to public ministry when He saw the multitude again. It is what is expected in merciful persons:

- from the physician who has served patients the livelong day, to serve still another patient;
- from the minister who, serving the flock the livelong day, to serve still another caller;
- from the parent serving children the livelong day, to serve still another child.

All these show mercy even when energy is believed to be used up.

Mercy is related to sensitivity. The ability to feel empathy for others must be an ideal mercy. Perhaps this is part of the story that Sheldon Vanauken meant to convey in his book, *A Severe Mercy*. He felt the mercy when he was most fully identified with his desperately ill wife and the two of them committed themselves to God. In that mercy Vanauken could receive his wife's fear of death and she could be at least partially relieved in relating to his ongoing life.

Through the centuries there have been great differences in mercy-showing by members of the Church. Feeling concern, mature Christians identify a greater number of needs to serve than those who are less compassionate. In studying the movements of history, one is impressed by the sensitivity of some Christians toward others, like slaves, and the lack of it in others who owned slaves and defended the institution. Across the centuries, Christians have differed in how they show mercy. Some owned slaves and others tried to free them. Slavery was prevalent in the early Church, a carry over from the general society. The apostle Paul wrote his friend Philemon to accept his runaway slave Onesimus as a brother, not a slave.

The Scriptures indicate that good fruits result from the work of merciful persons. This is a reminder of the biblical concept of mercy-showing, a spiritual gift. In nature, fruit is the final result of action in planting, tending and harvesting. It is possible to plant and tend, but receive no harvest. The indication here is that mercy will always end in harvest. The section on maturity appearing in the first chapter of Second Peter indicates the same result. Even David, the poet, related forgiveness to mercy, and forgiveness to harvest in Psalm 51.

Harvest is ultimately dependent upon the Giver of weather and water. With all the work of man, the harvest is dependent upon gifts of water and sun. Spiritual harvest is dependent upon the reproduction of God's mercy showered in the mercy of Christians.

The results of showing mercy must be good fruits. Without the arrogance demonstrated by others in his position, the centurion of Acts 10, in the experience of Peter, provides a relevant lesson. The centurion was honored, in part, because of his mercy to Jews. When the apostle Peter received the vision of the sheet filled with clean and unclean animals, he was being prepared to be a shower of mercy.

Peter also needed a reminder to be less parochial in how he showed mercy. At first, he believed God's love was intended only for the Jews—his countrymen. Receiving the vision of the sheet of mixed animals, Peter perceived that God would minister to Jews and Gentiles alike. In the experience, Peter gained the perception of mercy. Peter went directly to the centurion's home and introduced the Gentile man and his family to the gospel meant for every person. It was an experience that impressed Peter deeply for the rest of his life (see Acts 10).

The mature person who willingly demonstrates mercy serves others without thoughts of advancing his own personal treasury, status or honor. He is satisfied to feel that God has been served. He knows that when he serves others, he is doing what God does: God serves. God serves even those who do not serve Him in return, and the merciful person does likewise. It is the perfect altruism, service without any expectation of return.

The Christian Should Be Impartial, Therefore without Hypocrisy

A policeman on traffic duty one evening noticed a familiar automobile failing to stop at a marked intersection. Although ordinarily he would have immediately pursued the offender, this time he hesitated. He recognized the car as belonging to his favorite former high school English teacher, Miss Green.

After wrestling with himself for a moment, the young policeman obeyed his conscience and stopped Miss Green. He wrote out the ticket. As he handed it to her, he explained her infraction to her in terms he knew she would understand: "That was a period on the turn, Miss Green, not a comma."

Like the young policeman, we are sometimes tempted to act partially. But such partiality is wrong, and leads to hypocrisy, as suggested by the passage from James. When people act impartially, they act with integrity. They are so concerned with this character trait they avoid even the appearance of partiality. For this reason, trustworthy judges disqualify themselves rather than risk appearing partial in any case where they might have some connection or bias. Wise public servants take pains to avoid showing partiality to anyone, especially to their friends and family. Serious students will learn to be impartial in order to be open to truth. Without such impartiality, would-be scholars may refuse to go where the facts lead them.

Jesus was impartial in His treatment of others. On one occasion, He was addressing a crowd when told that His mother and brothers were at the door desiring to speak with Him. Instead of leaving immediately to meet with them, He replied, "Who is my mother, and who are my brothers?" Pointing to His disciples He said, "Here are my mother and my brothers" (Matthew 12:48-49).

Even though his biological family may have been offended, Jesus did not show partiality to the delegation. Jesus would, in proper time, give His family His attention. Their interests would be attended to. There was no need to close the meeting early. If traditional interpretation is valid, the family may have been testing His loyalty by creating dissonance between themselves, the crowd and Jesus. Jesus rejected the pattern. If their purpose was to rescue Him from an exhausting schedule, He had the right of judgment on the matter. There was no disrespect in Jesus' response (see Matthew 12:46-50).

Impartial persons are persons of principle. They avoid, wherever possible, even an appearance of partiality. Fact and appearance are both important. We expect to be treated fairly by those with whom we have to do. Human institutions, like government, are best when constructed on equity. Christians may need some adjustment in their perception of God, who is evenhanded in His treatment of humanity. They need to divest themselves of the tendency to believe that God is more merciful and less stern with His followers than with others.

If one combines these several characteristics from James 3:17 in his or her life and experience, he or she exemplifies maturity in the Christian meaning of the word. These biblical characteristics relating wisdom to maturity include:

1. Purity that reveals itself in godly peace, leading to power;
2. Gentleness that reveals itself in readiness to respond to needs expressed (entreaty), leading to action;
3. Mercy-showing that reveals itself in sensitivity, leading to good works; and all accomplished with,
4. Impartiality that reveals itself in genuineness through the absence of hypocrisy, and all leading to integrity.

For any Christian to become mature in the practice of this wisdom is to become Christlike. Christlikeness is the ultimate goal of the mature Christian.

_____ *Chapter*

_____ *6*

Values That Form Us

According as his divine power hath given unto us all things that pertain unto life and godliness, through the knowledge of him that hath called us to glory and virtue: Whereby are given unto us exceeding great and precious promises: that by these ye might be partakers of the divine nature, having escaped the corruption that is in the world through lust.

And beside this, giving all diligence, add to your faith virtue; and to virtue knowledge; And to knowledge temperance; and to temperance patience; and to patience godliness; And to godliness brotherly kindness; and to brotherly kindness charity. For if these things be in you, and abound, they make you that ye shall neither be barren nor unfruitful in the knowledge of our Lord Jesus Christ. But he that lacketh these things is blind, and cannot see afar off, and hath forgotten that he was purged from his old sins.

Wherefore the rather, brethren, give diligence to make your calling and election sure: for if ye do these things, ye shall never fall: For so an entrance shall be ministered unto you abundantly into the everlasting kingdom of our Lord and Saviour Jesus Christ. (2 Peter 1:3-11 KJV)

In his book *Hide or Seek,* James Dobson summarized the life of Lee Harvey Oswald, assassin of President John F. Kennedy in Dallas, Texas, in 1963. He described the tragic Oswald as an unlovely, unloved, incorrigible, lonely man, who failed in virtually everything he ever tried except for rifle marksmanship. He won infamy by using his single skill to murder the President of the United States. Dobson attributed Oswald's moral failure in part to being reared in a life context largely devoid of standard values that build character, esteem and family.

The matter of values, especially Christian values, and how to generate them in practical conduct is the focus of this chapter. Christian values contrast sharply with the values society maintains, so we must learn to differentiate.

Every culture has its own set of values which it may analyze in terms of continua. There may be a continuum that has beauty at one end and ugliness at another, genius at one extreme and retardation at the other, or various continua of values deemed important by that society. In *Hide or Seek,* Dobson reviewed two of the popular values in America: beauty and intelligence. Beauty he labeled the "gold coin" of American values, and intelligence he called the "silver coin."

In his analysis, Dobson suggested that members of the population, even inadvertently sometimes, are aware of the continuum of beauty, and would wish to believe themselves beautiful. The same applies to intelligence. It is interesting to note that in a 1992 Harris Poll conducted for the March of Dimes, respondents gave their highest approval for genetic experiments aimed at improving a child's physical characteristics (43 percent), with improving intelligence coming in right behind (42 percent).[1] Interestingly, the matter of improving morality was not addressed.

A distorted view of beauty may begin early in life when children inadvertently allow the messages of the classic nursery rhymes and children's stories to shape their feelings and thoughts about beauty. Consider some of these familiar titles: "The Ugly Duckling," "Rudolph, the Red-Nosed Reindeer," "Cinderella," "Snow White," "Dumbo the Flying Elephant" and "Sleeping Beauty." Sleeping Beauty, for example, remains beautiful after 99 years of sleep, and can only be awakened by the kiss of a handsome prince. He has to be handsome.

There are many similar stories, and they generally teach that being beautiful is being good or having authority and power. Ugliness, on the other hand, equates with badness, sadness, menial treatment, even death. The implication: homely persons are not good. And life experience seems to bear out this distortion of values.

Before they are very old, children learn the importance adults place on beauty. The most attractive children tend to get the best grades in school. They are treated with kinder words and greater acceptance than less attractive children. If a child is "bad," he may believe himself to be ugly, or, believing himself to be ugly, he may decide he is also bad. He may ultimately believe he is his group's "ugly duckling." The illusion of ugly/bad or bad/ugly extends to later years. Research in the field shows that prison inmates by and large do not perceive themselves to be physically attractive.

In a home for orphans, I watched once, many years ago, the way in which every Friday the children were presented to prospective adoptive parents. The children would walk through a room where they were observed for consideration. A blond, blue-eyed little girl walked through just once, and was adopted. But a lad with the strawberry mark down the side of his face was never spoken for. Such is society's focus on beauty. The less-than-perfect child who needed parents most was not chosen. That lad was a candidate for future antisocial behavior. If nothing better was done for him, he may have ended up in prison, like others in similar situations.

David Lavoie, murderer from Montreal, killed 15 persons in cold blood and assisted in 34 other murders. He blamed his behavior on the split-up of his parents that sent him to an orphanage. He believed himself to have been unattractive to adults. He assumed that his parents must not have loved him, and he said the lack of love made him incorrigible. Perhaps he overstated his case, but what he said may have some validity.

Dobson's silver coin is intelligence. Parents commonly speak of their children as being precocious, well above average. The parents seem to place greater value on children they perceive to be highly intelligent than on those of supposed lesser intelligence. Intelligence is so important to parents that average children are now perceived by their parents to be near genius. Evaluation is distorted. We are told that "grade inflation" takes place in colleges and universities because so many "must" get high grades—whether earned or not.

When I was teaching I noticed how parents in general perceived their children as gifted, whether or not they had any grounds for such evaluation. When parents brought their college-bound youths to campus early in September, they met faculty members at a reception which was part of the orientation activities. As their embarrassed son or daughter stood by, they extolled his or her potential, though they sometimes admitted that the young person's high school scholarship and discipline might not warrant such an evaluation. If the student's records did not prove the parents' high view of his or her ability, there was always an excuse: the high school was not as efficient as it should have been; the teachers were not dedicated; the courses were boring. Evidence shows, however, that in general, poor performance was more likely due to home influences that permitted excessive television viewing or other distractions—anything from family feuds to interminable, loud rock music, or even free use of an automobile. (Several studies show direct correlation of the free use of vehicles to reduction in academic performance.)

In many of these homes, too, family activity included virtually nothing in terms of relevant reading or meaningful discussion. A boy will not easily believe that reading is highly beneficial to his life when he never observes his father reading a substantive book or even an article from a first-rate periodical. Father implies, even if he does not state the case, that he is successful and adjusted in life. Why should the son, to match father's accomplishments, do what his father does not do?

Raw intelligence is not nearly so important as what one does with it, regardless of the importance society places on grades and test scores. When our three older children took the Washington Grade Prediction Test, they discovered that they scored in the middle range of those tested. Our children shared with us their doubts about how they would perform in college. I showed them the statement on the cover of the examination that said something to the effect that "This test cannot predict the academic performance of a student who applies himself." And that statement proved true. Our children performed well in college, at least in part because, not confident of any great intellectual endowments, they were dutiful to their studies.

Sometimes no amount of effort will result in academic success. When a child does not accomplish what families with high achievement traditions expect, tension and disappointment among family members may arise. Often that disappointment seems to them justified, even when a problem like retardation is the cause. Many of these families seem to feel that the family's reputation has been diminished or tarnished in some way. Their focus is not on maturity related to circumstances, but rather on family pride.

Certainly society does place stress on beauty and intelligence, but at least one more coin should be added to Dobson's collection—the coin of materialism. Every culture has its own range of wealth and poverty. In American culture, and only slightly less in Canadian, materialism dominates much of life.

When certain persons enter a room, they instantly convey an image of their wealth or influence (or of the illusions of these qualities). These impressive men and women are afforded privilege. People are drawn to wealth. Even in families, members divide between rich uncles and poor ones. An individual is treated a certain way by other family members based on the way they view his or her financial standing in relation to their own. Poor relatives place expectations on rich ones, expectations that often go far beyond the actual powers of their wealth or influence. Wealthy members have good reason to wonder, sometimes, whether they are appreciated for themselves or what they possess.

Nearly everything in the English-speaking world, especially the United States, is evaluated in the terms of dollars. Refugees often remark that the country they left emphasized homely values, while their new country, the United States, seems to them to have only one value—materialism. Many refugees say they would be pleased to be back in their own country if power politics and abject poverty did not prevent their return. They do not believe that improved living standards are fair exchange for life qualities. Nevertheless, in a short time, many of them are also caught up in the race for riches.

Emerging generations believe that wealth should be self-perpetuating. Although the first generation may have to make great sacrifices to achieve a degree of prosperity, the second generation does not have to work so hard. Still, the second generation often holds on to the values they admired in their parents. The third or fourth generation often loses the early perception of values attached to prosperity. They seem to think that one is entitled to the good life simply because he or she is an American or Canadian and alive. The work ethic is diluted, but expectations remain high and may even go higher.

Populations everywhere want what money can buy. Most persons work for money, but many hope for inheritances and windfalls along the way. Some hope to get money from begging, gambling or from crimes ranging from thievery to tax evasion. Theft is common, touching the majority of families in one way or another. Or, the love of money can lead to major crimes of embezzlement, drug running, piracy or even murder for profit.

Although our culture seems to think that wealth is everything, what or how much one owns is not really the issue. The issues are: 1) the attitude one holds toward wealth and its priority in things, and 2) the stewardship of material wealth, since wealth can be an effective tool for service. Affluent persons are not put down in the Scriptures, but they are called to use their possessions generously and to minister. Both the rich and the poor can be faithful in the use of their material goods—much or little.

Christian Values

In the text presented at the beginning of this chapter, the apostle Peter lists eight values related to Christian thought and practice. He wrote that when we make these priorities our regular practice, we may expect remarkable results. The values he listed are: faith, virtue, knowledge, temperance, patience, godliness, brotherly kindness and love. He did not imply that the list is exhaustive, but he did propose enough to keep serious Christians busy.

Each of these values could be seen as a continuum. A continuum places opposite values at each end of a line, permitting those who use the scale to judge approximate percentages for each position along the way. No one can measure accurately these percentages as they relate to human behavior—only God can measure such a matter. But the continuum provides a tool to show individuals the degree to which they may possess certain positive or negative qualities. When used, it gives an important point of reference. "Each one should test his own actions. Then he can take pride in himself, without comparing himself to somebody else" (Galatians 6:4).

Faith

There is a continuum of faith and unbelief.

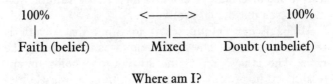

Where am I?

When we analyze our faith, we will often find that some doubt remains, at least related to some issues. The existence of some doubt, as Augustine taught, does not mean we are devoid of spiritual life and some effectiveness. But it does mean that to the degree that doubt exists, we are not functioning at the spiritual level we might be. By generating greater faith, a Christian improves his or her confidence and demonstrates a more effective spiritual life. The maturing Christian will sense fulfillment as he or she moves away from doubt and toward total belief.

The statements people make can provide a reasonable idea of where they stand on the faith-doubt continuum. Consider these statements people often make and how they relate to faith:

> "I do not believe in a personal God."
> "I don't believe my dad believes in anything."
> "There may be a God, but what I do means nothing to Him."
> "I really believed in God once; I am not sure that I believe now."
> "I am angry at God for what has happened to me."
> "I feel that God takes care of the big things and leaves the small things to us."
> "I believe you acknowledge Christ and His salvation, then learn to live in the real world."

"I believe that faith is as legitimate a way to learn as any other, and by faith I know the reality of God's salvation in Jesus Christ through whom I have eternal life."

"I believe through faith that God, in Christ, cares for me personally, and, as I am enabled, my life models that belief."

Spiritually-minded individuals could place each of these statements along a continuum between total faith in God and total unbelief. More importantly, we need to evaluate our own statements and beliefs. The apostle Peter clearly desired that his readers improve themselves in the direction of the values he listed. He began the listing with faith. Faith, as discussed earlier, is vital, utterly vital, for all Christians. It is the end of the continuum toward which the mature Christian is consciously moving.

Righteousness

There is a continuum of righteousness and evil.

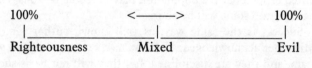

Where am I?

Those persons practicing Christian virtue are concerned with righteousness, fidelity, honesty, duty, responsibility and mercy. Those with less virtue will display, to some degree, infidelity, dishonesty, disrespect of duty, disregard of responsibility and lack of mercy. We are addressing here Christian righteousness. Other religions may advance what they call virtue but what, in Christianity, is evil. For example, the murder of neighbors who are infidels may be a virtue in some religions. In Christianity, however, the murder of any person is evil.

From the apostle Peter's first letter, we learn that Christians who progress toward the righteousness end of the continuum may, by their worthy conduct, draw attention to the good in life (see 3:13-17). Peter implied that every Christian may find and practice these values, if he or she chooses to do so. Virtue is not limited to specially gifted or highly educated Christians. The simplest person, if he or she is a Christian, may practice virtues that equal or surpass those of a genius who is also a Christian. The simple Christian may accept straightforwardly the Christian way, while the intellectual may be tempted to dilute biblical injunctions or redefine them, modifying virtue to his or her own preferences.

The Christian system of values stands in contrast to other systems of values in that in the Christian system, every individual can benefit without loss to anyone else. In God's economy, all persons can be spiritually rich, or, if they prefer, all can be spiritually poor—or somewhere in between. But in the natural system, for one person to be enriched, another may become impoverished. No matter how gifted or talented the population may be, some persons will be rich, and some will be poor.

Success is the same way, as well-known author James Michener acknowledged: "I know many writers as good as I am, and they are disciplined, but they will not be as successful because they were not and are not as lucky as I am." Michener knew that there is only so much room for successful authors, and those who are successful must, perforce, displace others.

Mature persons will resist the urge to measure themselves by society's values. Instead, they will seek the values that emanate from God. These are enriching, satisfying values, available to any and all who seek spiritually valued tender. With that exchange, persons may enrich those around them and impoverish no one.

Knowledge

There is also a continuum of knowledge and ignorance.

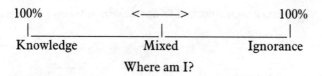

Where am I?

While society places high value on intelligence, spiritual knowledge is of major importance to the maturing Christian. Infants are born with a degree of intelligence, but they are not born with anything more than prenatal knowledge. As far as knowledge is concerned, we all start at the same place—we are all born in relative ignorance. But as infants mature, they increase in knowledge which helps them to function well in their world. And as Christians mature, they should be growing in knowledge that helps them to function well in their spiritual lives. This knowledge is largely gained from a study of the Bible, which provides a solid, logical basis upon which persons may pattern their beliefs and conduct.

Action is key. Only as a person applies knowledge can he or she gain more. When knowledge, whether spiritual or natural, is acted upon favorably, more knowledge presents itself as surely as a second mile becomes possible only to those who traverse the first. Steps cannot be skipped, but some participants are more swift than others in covering the necessary distance.

Ignorance, at one end of the spectrum, is among the most knotty of humanity's problems. Ignorance prevents us from solving problems. The worst kind of ignorance is that of pride, which pits human knowledge against God's. But there is also human laziness that results in apathetic attitudes toward spiritual growth, or even intellectual growth. Such laziness avoids searching for God. But mature persons seek knowledge, and adjust their conduct to what they find. The Scripture refers to spiritual knowledge as "true knowledge."

Temperance

There is a continuum of temperance and license.

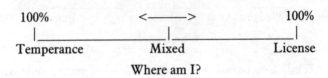

Where am I?

The opposite end of the continuum from license is not total self-denial, but temperance. Temperance is the balance between all and none. When we are moderate, we avoid overusing or underusing what is available. Temperance enjoys creation without abusing it or ourselves.

License, on the negative side, is displayed in drunkenness, gluttony, in the excess of any thing, even religion. Religiosity is a kind of intemperance, a distortion. The Scriptures warn about the matter even in reference to prayer. We are warned to avoid "babbling like pagans [who] think they will be heard because of their many words" (Matthew 6:7).

Intemperance commonly becomes the norm. Some erroneously use statistical averages to discover the temperate life, not realizing these averages are often already skewed toward license. A national average for body weights, for example, is determined by the weight of all divided by the number of subjects questioned. If the general population tends toward gluttony, then the average may well be evidence of intemperance, and therefore a poor guideline by which to judge body weight. Mature people must become masters of their own temperance.

Patience

There is a continuum between patience and impatience.

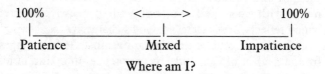

Patience in a person is evidence of self-control. Impatient persons too readily react to conduct of others that does not mesh with their own. Because so much conduct in others does not synchronize with ours, we can quickly test our level of patience.

Patience is expected from persons who are mature, as we expect it from parents interacting with their children. Patient persons act grown up. They are aware that the immediate event is not the end of things. Matters will be better tomorrow or next week. There is no need to overreact. It will take years to form the infant into a child, the child into an adolescent, the adolescent into an adult and the adult into a mature person. Patient men and women tend to become more aware of the wholeness of life, and are inclined to problem-solving.

Those who are impatient are often lacking in other values like faith and self-control. They tend to react to problems rather than solve them. Impatience marks the child; patience, the mature adult.

Godliness

There is a continuum of godliness and ungodliness.

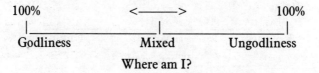

Godliness includes personal virtue, evidence of characteristics related to Christlikeness. It begins with an awareness of God that leads to awe and worship. The godly person makes an effort to live righteously, evading carnal thought and conduct. Even so, the concern here is not so much with good and evil, but with personal character which reflects, even relates to, God's character.

Ungodliness centers in rebellion against God. It ranges from a neglect of God and His preferences to a kind of ferocity in some persons who do not believe in God but are angry at Him for "not existing." Even references to God trigger ill feelings in them, perhaps venomous reactions. Prayer is disdained; every church is a leech on society. This is a common public response in some atheistic movements. Their activism has generated legislation favorable to their views. Some are almost violent when discussing a God they perceive as too unloving or powerless to intervene in situations they believe are tragic to humankind. They may even lash out against general, legitimate conduct, accepted as appropriate in a free society.

No negative response should deter genuine Christian conduct and belief, even when such activity creates enemies. Even God does not expect approval from all men and women, for either Himself or His people. He manages matters well, and so should the Christian. To receive broad approval would likely be an evidence of failure by the devout to maintain standards. All Christians should maintain love for their enemies, no matter the circumstances or consequences.

Kindness

There is a continuum of kindness and unkindness.

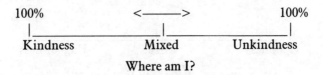

A kind person accepts others whether they are wrong, weak, noisy, ignorant or whatever. Kind persons never wish to see anyone excluded simply for personal reasons. Kind men and women are safe to be around. We can reveal ourselves without the fear of ostracism. Kindness, we readily sense, is a sign of maturity. We see it in its simplest form when an adult works patiently with a boisterous, slow-to-learn or fearful child.

Unkind persons, on the other hand, prefer to have weak, wrong, or unlikeable people out of the way. Unkind men and women, even children, are not safe to be around. There is nothing in the unkind person to inspire. There is little or no reciprocity or fairness. If logical they would be kind if for no better reason than that they will need kindness for themselves in the future. The unkind person often takes without giving back.

Job, characterized frequently for his patience, was also a kind person, as demonstrated by his concern for the slave, the poor, the widow, the orphan, the ill-clothed, the hungry, the accused, the innocent, the stranger. He did not so much as speak ill of an avowed enemy (Job 31:29-30). He was understandably perplexed, then, when his friends did not act kindly toward him in his sufferings. But like Job, the mature believer will be kind to others, even when that kindness is not returned.

Love

There is a continuum of love and hate.

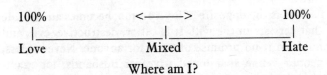

Where am I?

Loving persons are special people. Any family with loving persons among its members is greatly blessed. Loving people are pleasing to be around because they control their will in order to act and believe in unselfish and Christlike ways.

The love Peter indicated in this text is not the love that is so familiar in the current culture. "In love" romance is ephemeral, dissolving when one member or the other fails in a relationship. The Greek word *agape*, used often in the Scriptures, finds its meaning in the unselfish nature of the lover, not in the object of that unconditional love. Another Greek word for love, *eros* relates to human passion. *Eros*, in its original meaning, was noble for its purpose, but is too narrow for mature love. *Eros* finds its attraction in the love object, not in the character of the lover.

Even the Greek word *phileo*, which implies a natural and useful kind of reciprocal love, is too narrow. The apostle Peter was writing about *agape* love in this context — defined in First Corinthians 13. Such love is mature, shining upon and blessing all who share in the life of the loving person. In a population strong with self-interest, this kind of love is in short supply.

Because the topic of love has been treated often and well, it will be passed over with the few remarks made here. But let there be no doubt that love is indispensable to maturity. Even society in general relates love to maturity, as suggested by the results of a study reported in *Psychology Today:* "We found that when parents—particularly mothers—really loved their children, the sons and daughters were likely to achieve the highest levels of social and moral maturity."[2] How much more important is love to the development of Christian maturity.

Hate is the opposite of love. It, too, becomes an attitude that persists in the will. It is bitter, destructive, evil, and holds in it no promise of good for anyone. Nevertheless, people—some abandoned wives or husbands, for example—do sometimes turn to it, hoping to find solace. But hatred, often carried out in revenge, offers only false hope for peace. Hatred always results in bitterness, which becomes its own punishment. Hatred degrades the bitter person who clings to it as though it were the only satisfaction available. Love, on the other hand, uplifts not only the lover, but also the one who is loved. And it leads to maturity among those who practice it.

We have briefly reviewed the eight values Peter outlined as essential to mature Christian living. At this point some may find that the idea of Christian maturity seems too difficult. For others, it may seem too complex. It is neither, although it is true that personal development is hard work—it is extensive and time-consuming. The features of maturity are clear enough, and every Christian has the assistance of the Holy Spirit to make them achievable. It is very important—and cannot be overemphasized—that even a small increment in improvement makes a large difference.

Mature Christians will cultivate the values Peter listed in combination to make up a gracious spiritual life. But to simplify matters, it is helpful to consider each of the values separately. Christians who find themselves well along in some factors, partially along in others, and barely begun in still others, need to devote themselves to those features nagging for attention. Christians strong in faith but short on kindness ought to give serious attention to the cultivation of kindness. Strong in temperance, they may need help in developing patience. Each person should make his or her own diagnosis and then proceed by prescribing improvements for him or herself, learning from both successful and unsuccessful experiences, from models and biblical concepts. Such a person is headed toward maturity.

The P.A.C.E. Principles

In the context of values there are patterns of conduct which turn into habits and move the Christian in the right direction on the various continua. These patterns can become a way of life. Cast in an acrostic, they make up the P.A.C.E. principles: Prayer, Acceptance, Communication and Example. Each is divided into two parts and, when applied, can serve well in one's search for personal, Christian maturity. The following presents something of a summary of their personal applications in my observation of experience and personal life.

Prayer

Prayer can be divided into two kinds—public and private—but even church members do not give much thought to either, especially private prayer. For many churchgoers, prayer is perceived as something that the pastor does at some point in the church service. Public prayer, then, is sincere, worshipful, general, and it usually follows a formula of address, adoration, confession, assurance, petition, hope and benediction. Some church members seem satisfied that they have all the prayer they need if they hear the pastoral prayer on Sundays and recite a paragraph for grace at mealtimes—tossing in the Lord's Prayer on formal occasions or as a substitute for personal prayer.

In his book *Christian Maturity*, E. Stanley Jones said that this is not enough. Jones challenged Christians to regular, personal prayer because as he traveled and talked to Christians from many different backgrounds and cultures, he found that the "greatest source of weakness in character and influence is to be found in the prayer life." He believed that most of "the casualties in the spiritual life" are related to weakened prayer activity. "Prayer is pivotal," he affirmed.

Jones observed a direct correlation between his personal quality of life and the amount of time he spent in prayer. When he was prayerful, he said he felt like an illuminated light bulb fixed firmly in its socket. But when he lacked prayer, he said he felt like a light bulb pulled out of its socket. For Jones, a person is no more likely to be vital spiritually without prayer than a light bulb is to produce light without being connected to its energy source.

Private prayer addresses personal needs and is therefore more individual than public prayer. The most effective prayer I ever remember praying was a simple two words: "Oh, God." I repeated them numerous times over the space of a number of minutes. They flowed up from deep inside me like hot heavy lava. If others had been present, they probably would not have been comfortable listening to my prayer, but I was not praying for others. I was praying to God and only to God. And God heard and answered that simple, heartfelt prayer, providing me with peace and comfort.

Prayer may have broader uses than most persons imagine. On one occasion I was so angered by the unsatisfactory conduct of one of my children that when he later made strong protest to me, I asked him to pray for me. I told him I felt ill will toward him, and was angry at his attitude. After additional protest, he acquiesced. Before continuing long into the prayer, he was praying for himself. The experience changed him in dramatic ways, perhaps changed me as well. Civility was never lost in our exchanges thereafter.

For mature Christians, prayer—especially brief, private prayers expressed throughout the day—becomes a way of life. Anything in their lives can be immediately, sincerely and intensely (or casually, depending on circumstances) touched by prayer. They are prayerful about family relationships, a trip in the car, a backache or whatever else may be on their minds. They freely pray in the night when they awaken and sleep eludes them. There is a kind of prayerful trust that is as common to them as the air they breathe.

Acceptance

Acceptance has two facets: self-acceptance and acceptance of others. But the acceptance of others is related to self-acceptance. If people cannot accept themselves, they will have distorted, often excessively high expectations of others, yet they hold themselves in reserve to avoid the possibility, or illusion, of failure. Relationships commonly warp because of distorted perceptions of self and others.

A person's age, body size, geographic location, profession, competence, health, education and faith—all may factor into one's degree of self-acceptance. Within boundaries, we must learn to like who we are, not wishing to be someone else.

At the close of a summer conference, a lady asked for counsel. When she and her husband arrived at our cabin, my wife offered them seats on the couch. The woman took the extreme end to the left, her husband sat far right, leaving a space between them that seemed like a canyon. My wife and I sat on chairs opposite the couple.

"He won't let me have a nose job," the woman said hooking her thumb toward her husband. "And he can afford it."

"You wish to have plastic surgery on your nose?" I asked.

"Yes, an eighth of an inch off the end of my nose."

Turning to her husband, I asked his opinion.

"She is the most beautiful woman I have ever seen. I like her just the way she is, and so do the children," he said. "This thing is hurting our family. I don't want her to do it, and the children don't like it either. This whole thing focuses too much on a matter unsuitable to what we stand for. There is too much accent on a body and face. God gave her what she's got."

I asked the woman if she had any other problems.

"My thighs are too thick," she retorted.

I determined not to talk about that, so I went back to discussing her nose. "Give me your right profile," I requested.

She turned her face slightly left. I repeated the request for the opposite profile. My wife and I both noticed that the woman was quite attractive and exuded a picture of good health. While cosmetic surgery might well be indicated for some persons, especially for those disfigured in some way, strong objections to such surgery from loving family members might mean that the person was putting too much emphasis in some areas, and too little in others.

For this woman, the higher Christian values were not in place. She was immature. Her desire to be "someone else" prevented her from gaining self-acceptance and denied easy acceptance of her by her husband and children.

Communication

Communication also involves two kinds: sending and receiving. One depends on the other. But while there appears to be no lack of senders, listening appears to be a weak art in interpersonal relationships. Mature people will work to master effective listening skills. In so doing they will serve both themselves and others.

One of the most poignant stories I ever heard was told by my wife about an incident that happened to her when she was in junior high school. One day was dark for some particular reason—an injustice long since forgotten. Perhaps a boy pulled her curls, or a teacher misunderstood her conduct, or a test did not go as well as expected. Whatever the cause, my wife tried to tell her mother about the event. But her mother moved from room to room as though escaping her daughter's incessant conversation. She pursued, and her mother, still on the move, responded, "Uh huh," "Yeah," "Am-m-m," "Hm-m-m," "Yeah," "Uh-huh."

At last the daughter stopped, stood in the center of the living room and silently screamed, addressing her mother in her thoughts: "I will not tell you anything that means anything to me as long as I live." And she did not, until many years later.

Sometimes people feel that they must talk, so they simply talk. The mature person will not mind listening, and when the first person has said what he or she wishes to say, the listener, because he or she has listened well, will be able to respond meaningfully. The listener will better understand the facts and feelings of the other person because he or she has heard them fully. Such communication creates fewer opportunities for misunderstanding, error and offense. The listener will be wiser, and he or she will speak to persons who respect what he or she has to say, because he or she has first listened to them. The mature listener tends to cultivate four skills: greeting (recognizing the speaker), healing (considering the emotional state of the speaker), finding (discovering the relevant facts) and evaluating (suggesting what needs to follow). Effective communication is a mark of the mature person.

Example

Example is of two kinds: biblical and personal. Personal example, or modeling, is well known. Even though a Christian principle, it is also universal among civilizations. Pagan tribes expect tribal members to model their values, just as teachers in ancient Greece and Rome made modeling a major feature of family and formal education. It was vital in the law of Israel, and remains in Christian teachings. Moses instructed the Israelites to teach their children by example, and Paul urged believers to follow him in the way he followed Christ.

The principle is basic: If we want to teach our children to avoid lying, we must not lie. If we want them to refrain from stealing, we also refrain from stealing. Positive values are taught in affirmative modeling. We teach the value of work by working, the value of kindness by being kind, and the value of giving by giving ourselves and gifts to others.

Mature people both lead and follow. Both are done best by those who believe in modeling. Effective following is vital to effective leading. Maturing Christians find examples in other mature Christians, and they find examples from the Scriptures. Some biblical examples are affirmative (Joseph, Abigail, Nehemiah, Paul) and some negative (Ahab, Herod, Demas). Either way, these biblical characters provide valuable models for cultivating maturity.

When daughters-in-law were added to our family, I knew that I wanted to gain rapport, show love, and encourage family solidarity with them. I did what I had done before in situations where I wanted an example to follow—I went to the Scriptures. In the past I had found models there for marriage, ministry, friendship, stewardship, parenting and what have you. Surely there would be a model for fathers-in-law.

For my in-law father lesson, I found Jethro, father-in-law to Moses. He seems to have been as nearly perfect a father and father-in-law as one may find. Admittedly the narrative is sketchy, but there is enough of the story for the purpose. From that story, one finds that Jethro's treatment of Moses could not be much improved upon. He did many positive things including the reconciliation of Moses with Zipporah. He offered wise counsel for the governing of God's people in the wilderness. Jethro appeared ready to assist wherever he could, and was unwilling to become a burden to anyone.

With Jethro in mind, I determined to do what I could to develop good relationships with our children's mates. I found myself speculating about what Jethro might have done in modern circumstances. I felt he would have done whatever he could to keep child and spouse together. He would not have interfered, but he would have been available. He would have assisted when matters became difficult, if assistance was appropriate. He would have been friendly and objectively concerned. But he would have bowed out when his participation was no longer needed. With such lessons from Jethro, I occupied myself to become an acceptable father-in-law.

Putting into practice what I was learning, I took my daughter-in-law out to lunch one afternoon. We talked the whole time about her husband, my son. After lunch I asked her if she was in a hurry to be someplace and since she was not, I took her to a mall and bought her a pants suit.

"There," I said. "Go home and model that for your husband, and say, 'This is what your dad purchased for me; now what do you have to offer?' " We laughed, and I took her home. That was the first of many other enjoyable exchanges, thanks to Jethro.

Scripture provides the models for all those who desire to grow to spiritual maturity. It provides examples for specific areas of Christian conduct, and, in its implications, is also useful for creating a "big picture" for Christian living.

Endnotes

1 Snider, Mike. "Many favor gene therapy to enhance babies," *USA Today*, September 29, 1992, sec. A, p. 13. Copyright USA Today. Reprinted with permission.

2 McClelland, David C., et al. "Making It To Maturity," *Psychology Today*, June 1978, p. 45. Reprinted with permission from *Psychology Today*. Copyright 1978 (Sussex Publishers, Inc.).

Chapter 7

Do You Have VIP?

Be patient, then, brothers, until the Lord's coming. See how the farmer waits for the land to yield its valuable crop and how patient he is for the autumn and spring rains. You too, be patient and stand firm, because the Lord's coming is near. Don't grumble against each other, brothers, or you will be judged. The Judge is standing at the door!

Brothers, as an example of patience in the face of suffering, take the prophets who spoke in the name of the Lord. As you know, we consider blessed those who have persevered. You have heard of Job's perseverance and have seen what the Lord finally brought about. The Lord is full of compassion and mercy. (James 5:7-11)

Frank Pace, a member of President Harry Truman's cabinet, was once asked what he believed made for personal success. His answer: "Vision! Integrity! Patience!"

Pace's statement succinctly expresses factors that are important for personal spiritual development. It is a simple formula for a full and effective life—vision, integrity, and patience, VIP. Like any important pattern for human conduct, VIP may be found in Christian principles traced out in the Scriptures. VIP forms a pattern useful in business, in church, in family, but especially in personal conduct.

Vision Is Perceiving the Future in the Present

"Where there is no vision, the people are unrestrained."
(Proverbs 29:18, NASB)
"[Y]oung men will see visions." (Joel 2:28)

Persons with vision are looking in the right direction—forward. It is obvious that they follow a vision instead of a fantasy because of the constructive way they conduct themselves in order to bring about the future they envision. Vision is often attributed to young people, and it is little wonder. Their earthly future is something they are counting on much more so than are their elders. Young men and women have more of the future in store for them, so it is reasonable to expect that they would extend their vision. The light shines in the world, farther ahead for them than for their elders.

Spiritual vision is the ability to see some future goal almost as though it were already achieved. It closely relates to Christian hope. Hope functions as though a future act is done—it is as good as history, except that it has not yet been verified. Vision is also closely related to achievement because achievements are made when appropriate procedures are applied to vision. By perceiving and doing—that is by seeing the future and accordingly taking action in the present—genuine spiritual vision is exercised.

Spiritual vision has its counterpart in humanistic vision, as accented in Pace's comments that opened this chapter. Although they are not likely to use Scripture to support their statements, the world's knowledgeable men and women understand that vision is necessary to success, as illustrated in a leading newsmagazine in 1990, which argued that Gorbachev was not likely to succeed in Russia. According to the article, Gorbachev's *perestroika* (restructuring) and *glasnost* (openness) seemed to fall back on him. "Gorbachev lacks the understanding and the vision needed for his main goal,"[1] it stated. In a matter of months the magazine's analysis proved correct—Gorbachev was out of office.

Canada's long standing debate over the status of French-speaking Quebec is another example of how vision or a lack of it can affect a nation. In the late 1980s, Quebec's people rallied again around their lingering vision to be independent. Canadian provinces proposed the 1987 Meech Lake Accord which would have federalized the nation while recognizing Quebec as a distinct society. But when the accord was voted on in 1990, it failed to gain the unanimous support of the 10 provinces required to ratify it.

Proponents of the accord writing in Canadian newspapers suggested that the effort failed because of a lack of vision on the part of the Canadian government countered by a presence of strong vision on the part of the Quebecers. Writing in the *Calgary Herald*, Bill Warden recalled French President Charles de Gaulle's statements during the Canadian Centenary in 1967 when de Gaulle suggested liberty and independence for Quebec. Although de Gaulle is deceased, his outspoken views represented an ongoing dream for many Quebecers. Warden believed the accord failed because de Gaulle planted in Quebec "the vision of a Quebec destined to protect, preserve and promote its distinctiveness at all costs." That vision remained to stimulate Quebecers to think independently of provinces with English roots.

Warden commented that the dream to unite Canada with one parliament and one national anthem had failed "simply because this would require vision and statesmanship beyond the apparent ken of any political figure on the horizon today."[2]

In a letter written to the same newspaper another reader also used the word "vision" in expressing her disappointment over the failed accord. She wrote: "Our leaders lack vision and our people lack purpose."[3] During 1992 another proposal for national unification was rejected by Canadian representatives.

Theorists believe that vision is necessary in order to get needed results. The United States provides another example, among many. During 1992, incumbent President, George Bush, was defeated in national elections. Observers suggested that the President-elect, Bill Clinton, seemed to inspire national vision, whereas the incumbent did not. Bush was hurt in the elections because he had backed down on an important part of his vision from four years earlier relative to freedom and taxes. During 1994, when Clinton's party was overwhelmingly defeated at the polls, for the congressional elections, the analysts said that a major cause for the defeat was that the president had abandoned the vision articulated two years earlier, a vision that had won for him.

Illustrations can be stacked showing that vision is important for a nation, a business, a school, a church, or for an individual. Even when vision is present, it is not enough. When too little is done to achieve the objectives of the vision, it dissolves. If anything, the maker of the vision seems less capable than before the vision was articulated.

Although young people possess high potential for vision, they sometimes cut vision off simply by ignoring available opportunities and possibilities. Those who work with youths are often appalled at their lack of personal vision. Relatively few plan their lives with serious care.

Marshall McLuhan, the distinguished scholar of popular culture, held a view of youth and vision which, although popular, was not broadly factual. The youthful generation, according to McLuhan's metaphor, is looking through the windshield of life's automobile to the future. McLuhan said that the elders watch through the rear view mirror to the past, while members of the middle generation are sidelookers, glancing sideways through the door window, pre-occupied with the present. McLuhan made the common mistake of ascribing, almost automatically, vision to youthful generations.

Relatively few youths look, with the intent of guiding their lives, through the windshield of the future. And there are those in other age groups who do not confine themselves to looking out side windows or rear view mirrors. Any age group may look in any direction. One's age is not the issue. Vision belongs to the mature of any generation.

Men and women with effective personal vision feel compelled to draw life maps, even if sketchy at first. The purpose of drawing a life map is to accent attitudes, list needed resources and suggest actions. Such maps are imperfect, since they chart unexplored territory. They are vital, even though tentative, because vision is necessary to generate action. These personal maps usually do not plan for detours. Nevertheless, the map will be invaluable even in the event of a detour, because it keeps the destination clearly in view.

Virtually all men and women encounter detours. For those with vision, detours are temporary. They follow their maps to get back on track and continue toward desired goals. Unless persons set out with some sense of direction, their lives may bog down in delays and detours. For Christians, heaven is the final destination. They stay close to the biblical map to assure safe arrival.

A vision may include some perceptions of places, things and persons that the forward-looking individual may expect to encounter in the accomplishment of his or her goals. A faithful vision offers reasonable insights about future realities. If I am unsure of my road, I will at least know that I wish to go west. So I will travel in a westerly direction, moving closer to my goal. I have not been to this destination before, but perhaps friends and colleagues have, so I may ask them for directions. But I continue my vision, knowing that the more I give myself to it the greater is the likelihood that it will become reality.

The person with vision contrasts sharply to the one without vision. Many persons feel lost, and do not know why. If someone asks them where they are now, or where they are planning to go in the future, they shrug. Some admit that they felt lost on the journey from the moment they set out. They confess that they cannot tell the difference between a detour and a main highway. With no clear direction for them, all roads are equal, any direction is as good as another—north, east, south or west. They are hung up on little details that make traveling comfortable. They forgot to ask seriously, "Where are we going?" or "What direction does the goal indicate for us?" For them, the trip, not the destination, is virtually everything—"We don't know where we're going, but we're on our way, and trying to have fun getting there." However, research reported in 1995 showed that more than 40 percent of the population studied were deeply uneasy about themselves and society. The prevailing prosperity, full employment, and favorable environment were not enough. The analysts were surprised at the results, and noted the lack of personal vision in respondents.

For Christians the content of the vision involves a reasonable idea about God's program for the world, how it can be implemented, and what believers may do toward that end. But even Christian visionaries do not know everything about the plan. When asked about her vision, Mother Teresa said that it was good she did not know what the price of her vision would be, or she might have said "No" to Jesus. And the possibility that she might have said "No" to Jesus frightened her.

Vision is part of the stuff of prophecy, and prophets, when they are faithful, have faithful vision. In the Old Testament, a vision was most often a mental image of something, as in a dream, revelation or oracle, that enabled prophets to see into the future. The prophets did not always understand what they saw and heard. Nevertheless, they articulated their visions.

Vision as the word is used here is not as clearly defined as simply in Scripture as we might like. The word does appear a number of times, as noted in the texts that opened this section. Note Isaiah's writings, especially chapters 42 and 43. But the Scriptures tend to illustrate vision more than explain it. Abraham's vision took him into a promised land; Moses' vision was for the same land, and although he was not permitted to enter, Moses led Israel to its borders; Jeremiah, with the vision of the future of Israel, bought land during a period when the land was believed to be worthless (Jeremiah 32). Later, the land became valuable.

Vision integrates the past with the future in that it ties historical truths and ideals with the future. Part of the ancient prophetic vision was stimulated by concern that God's people would forget that which they should remember about the past. When members of an institution discuss its future, they usually review the past, especially the vision of the institution's fathers. If the institution departs from that first vision, there ought to be good reason for doing so. Not to give an accounting defies heritage. Those who show they can be responsible to their past will likely also be responsible for their future.

Human social tendencies move almost inevitably toward decline and decay. How can we preserve our ideals and the best from our past? Perhaps, we feel we have lost something, but do not know what. If this happens, we may have to trace back to the point where we left the road. The earlier vision, if it was good in the beginning, may be good now. It can help us to act in responsible ways now so as to slow any decline. Turnaround may come later when others take our place and have a heart for what needs to be done. At the very least, vision will protect us from losing our way completely.

Little wonder that the Bible records Israel observing so many special events in its history. If what the people had was of God, they dared not lose it. No other people seem so proud of their history or so competent in reminding their generations about national beginnings. An example of this vision is seen in the well-known Jewish farewell greeting: "Next year in Jerusalem." It is vision like this which kept Israel united despite centuries of living without a homeland. Israel is in Jerusalem today—the vision is reality.

Persons with vision know there is no other plausible direction in which to turn than to the future. The past is irretrievably lost and the present melts immediately into the past. But the present also flows into the future. So vision requires some goal setting or else we become as shortsighted as Peter emerging from the resurrection tomb of Jesus and announcing that he was going fishing (see John 21:3). His statement hardly qualifies as a satisfactory goal under the circumstances of Christ's resurrection. But Peter was a sleepy disciple. He slept in Gethsemane and at the transfiguration. Even on the night before he was scheduled to die, he was fast asleep, apparently not in any great distress (Acts 12). He was not easily awakened, either physically or spiritually.

Peter changed after Pentecost, when he received a vision—a dream of a sheet laden with clean and unclean animals. Before the vision he appeared often to be unsure, stalling in the drag of his own weaknesses. He was ambivalent and frustrated, reacting to experiences rather than thinking them through and acting constructively. But aroused at Pentecost, his vision focused and his work became fulfilling. It remains with us in his writings.

The past is like rock, the present like quicksilver, and the future like clay. The past is firm and set; nothing can change it except perhaps chipping away at it to make sculptures. The present is fast-moving and illusive. It slips through the fingers and so must be worked with in a crucible. People are usually clumsy with quicksilver and similarly they are clumsy with their days lived out in the present. But the future is palpable. The future can be molded. We have little to say about our past or present, but we have significant influence over the future.

Some people seem to resist their futures, their most important time dimension. They may become what eastern Canadians have called "everyday hosers"—ordinary guys—who live for "babes, beer, bacon and doughnuts." There is nothing in life that is remarkable for "hosers," nothing that inspires their future. Their kind live day by day, without goals or guidelines for their futures. They have no substantial commitment to direct their lives or their families. They just "hope for the best."

Many men and women, we discover, have vision for their futures, but in only a limited way. They may, for example, have detailed visions for their retirement. They may plan to buy property on which they will build their homes. They have planned their finances for that season of their lives, making sure they have ample insurance, stocks and bonds, and large enough savings accounts. They likely have a government retirement program, perhaps another with their company. They evaluate their needs at retirement age, and partially figure what they can do about health insurance, recreational interests and day-to-day living. They even have a particular retirement date in mind. They devote many hours and part of their present income to assure what they hope to experience for the 10 years or so that they will live after retirement.

The same persons who show great vision in the area of retirement may have no plans at all for immortality. They have no vision for greater things. Their lack of vision indicates weak belief, because what they believe in they plan for.

The international retailer Lanier Worldwide, Inc., understands vision. Lanier's leaders believe in making a profit, and they also believe that satisfied customers lead to those kinds of profits. Accordingly, they set out to make their customers happy. They developed what they call "Customer Vision," by which they discovered what their customers thought and expected of them. Then they set out to make those expectations into reality. The plan worked, as evidenced by sales increasing from one million dollars in 1955 to one billion dollars in 1990, operations moving from a few American states to 50 countries, and employees growing from a handful to 7,000.

The analogy is obvious—if I may discover what God expects of me, I have the best vision possible. The next step is simply "to make it happen." This takes place, at least in part, through integrity.

Integrity Is the Consistency of Good Persons

"But I did not do so because of the fear of God"
(Nehemiah 5:15, NASB).

Persons with integrity are honest about themselves. The public has become skeptical about the personal integrity of national figures because of publicized immoral exploits. If elected officials and other persons in respected positions of leadership break standards in their private, personal morality, what assurance does the electorate have that they would act differently with their public responsibilities?

It is difficult in our era to believe in the integrity of institutions when so many leaders have been the subjects of lurid exposés into their scams, alcoholism, sexual dalliance and the like. Some individuals even evade the laws they helped to pass. Not until 1995 were members of Congress required to keep the laws they passed for the common citizens of the country. Legislators would benefit by looking to Nehemiah to discover how a leader ought to conduct himself. Nehemiah acted with integrity—that is, without double standards or devious intent.

Although other governors had taken bread, wine and money from the people, Nehemiah refused to act as they did for good reason: He "feared the Lord." Nehemiah refused to ask for or accept bribes. With godly fear he relied upon Providence for his needs and the needs of the people.

Nehemiah was proud that his people were not on government welfare. He could have legally drawn government support for his entourage as they rebuilt Jerusalem, but he did not. To have done so would have added a burden to citizens already under heavy obligation and living in depressed times. People of integrity maintain clean motives and follow them for their own satisfaction as well as for the good of others.

Some analysts believe the public has been so disappointed with the widespread failure and scandal related to public servants, business people and celebrities, including some celebrated ministers, that there is a general decay of faith in both personal and civil life. These analysts believe the individual citizen may feel fairly good about him or herself, but has lost trust in others who have not kept integrity. However, evidence suggests that even common citizens may not be justified in feeling quite as they do about themselves since they too fall into unethical and immoral practices. There is flagrant pilferage, tax evasion, rights violations, infidelity and misuse of personal resources.

Part of the problem of understanding integrity relates to an inflation of the language we use to talk about ourselves. Football players often illustrate the point—they affirm their prowess as players, claiming they give 110 percent on the field. Of course that is impossible—no one gives more than 100 percent—but by inflating their competency, the less than total performer now claims he gives 100 percent, so competing players go outside of reality to express their belief that they are better than average. One columnist rightly asked, "Who is guilty of this language inflation?" He was not sure, but a commentator noted that athletes were outbidding each other on self-opinions. One report from an athlete claimed that he gave, "200 percent every time he carried the ball." That is arrogance—or maybe ignorance—or perhaps both. In any event, it is not being truthful.

We may inflate the language to try to express our competencies, but we are guilty of language deflation when it comes to assessing our failures. Much of what was once identified as evil is no longer called evil or sin, but rather "mistakes," or "errors in judgment," or "foibles." Instead of promiscuous, the term is now "sexually active." Even sexual excesses or aberrations are taken as illnesses, to be treated not as moral problems but as medical. In some instances, illness may indeed be a factor, but the moral side of the problem is usually neglected, even denied. And in some instances what used to be aberrations are now accepted as normal conduct with no excuses—they are called neither sin nor sickness. For example, homosexuality, which was defined as a serious psychological aberration and disease as late as the early 1970s, is currently considered normal and natural for those who choose to follow it. Little evidence was offered to justify the change in diagnosis. The population was expected to change, almost overnight, a view that the social analysts had insisted upon for centuries. Questioning homosexualtiy was suddenly shifted from objectivity to prejudice.

Whether sickness is involved or not, people of integrity take responsibility for their lives. They are not helpless victims. Mature men and women take responsibility for themselves, and they are objective in evaluating both personal strengths and weaknesses. They are truthful.

One might wonder what would have happened to his administration if Richard Nixon had been truthful early on in the Watergate scandal. What if he had acknowledged at the outset that his conduct and that of his associates was wrong, even sinful, and that he was sorry? But he refused to tell the truth when forgiveness would have been available. If he had, he could have perhaps avoided massive suffering in the political body. Instead, millions of citizens were lied to, while fierce protestations of innocence were made. What might have been a relatively minor problem was inflated to curse a nation. As the evidence piled up, the president lost his place with the people. He had sacrificed his integrity and resigned under pressure.

It is not only those in public life who sacrifice their integrity. Integrity can be lost over something so minor as a wrinkle on a face. In a published biography of a popular movie star, it was reported that the actress had said that while women should accept inevitable wrinkles, her physical fitness program would retard signs of aging. Her devotees saw in her the living proof of her program. What they did not know, according to the biographer, was that the woman underwent plastic surgery to assure her youthful appearance. She may have looked young, but her duplicity sacrificed her integrity. Since publication of the book, she acknowledged undergoing "the standard Hollywood alterations."

Persons with integrity know that inconsistency can lead to evil. Perhaps most persons oversimplify their understanding of evil. Many people seem to limit wrongdoing to the violation of selected commandments—adultery, thievery, profanity, lies and murder. But evil is not only the opposite of good; sometimes it is a good thing done for the wrong reason. To do good things for only as long as the money holds out, for example, is hardly virtuous conduct. Integrity has its own higher, consistent, motivation.

Our opinion of self-centered politicians is that they may do many things that are presumed beneficial, but that they do them cynically and with mixed motives. They do them in order to win votes. "That's politics," we are told. "Whitewashed tombs," Jesus said.

When we compromise integrity, we are like a double-image picture on the television screen. One image is brighter and fairly well defined, while the other is shadowy. We feel like two people—one good, one bad. This makes us uneasy. In Romans 7, the apostle Paul discussed the tension between his own good and evil desires. "I do not understand what I do," Paul wrote. "For what I want to do I do not do, but what I hate I do. . . . What a wretched man I am! Who will rescue me from this body of death?" (7:15, 24). So we fumble with the controls, trying to sharpen the image and bring it into focus. The person of integrity seeks one consistent image in his presentation. If we feel "double," we need better focus. Personal peace is related to personal integrity.

Integrity, then, is doing the right things for appropriate reasons, and doing them with consistency. It is a high standard, but it is the expected pattern of life. We should not feel proud if we have acted with integrity—we are merely doing what God expects of us. Persons who learn to act with integrity learn to sustain it through patience—the third factor of the VIP formula.

Patience Is Living Commitment through to Its Conclusion

"By standing firm you will gain life" (Luke 21:19).
"You too, be patient and stand firm" (James 5:8).
"You need to persevere" (Hebrews 10:36).
"He who stands firm to the end will be saved" (Matthew 10:22).

Persons who are patient are committed to complete what they set out to do. They are in for the long haul. For those who determine they will patiently finish out to the end, there are preliminary considerations related to the commitment:

1. They ought to feel that this is the right thing to do or believe.
2. They ought to hold that if there is a spiritual dimension in the matter there must also be a faith component in it.
3. They ought to believe that this action or belief is meant to give honor to God.
4. They ought to assume that humanity's estimations for how long the project will take are almost always wrong—a fact which relates to patience.

The Scriptures sometimes use agricultural word pictures to illustrate patience. The Epistle of James gives readers a picture of farming: farmers plant, then wait for harvest.

But farmers do not wait in idleness—they cultivate, they mulch, they chase predators. The analogy is especially meaningful to me because it brings back memories of pleasant childhood summers when I worked for a farmer. He worked hard, seeing to it that his fields, buildings and yard were well cared for, and his animals were the finest in the area. At times, when rain was scarce, he would nonetheless continue his labor, but I sometimes wondered why he bothered because it seemed all his hard work would be in vain. Without rain, after all, the wheat would dry up and the corn wilt. But the farmer pressed on with his vision for a crop, marking harvest dates on his calendar even when the tender wheat grass was barely above the ground.

I remember one day in particular. The farmer hurried us in from the field, so we could complete the barnyard chores early. He said it was going to rain, and that we needed to get the work done quickly because it would "rain hard." We did as directed and, chores finished, his son and I went into the house. The farmer, however, remained outside, standing on the stoop, looking westward toward the Wabash River. He stood there with his thumbs hooked in the galluses of his bib overalls, his face marked with an expression that looked like reverence. "It's going to rain hard," he said.

He stood there until the first few raindrops washed his skin, then, smiling, he entered the house. His patience was fulfilled—it "rained hard." That fall he harvested handsome crops for which he had worked and waited.

Many worthwhile pursuits require an investment of patience in order to enjoy the harvest. Parents, for example, invest years into their child. They do the best they can, and they season their efforts with prayer, but ultimately, Christian parents must learn simply to love and trust. That love and trust is sustained with patience, making the parents willing to await the results. A child may resist attempts to be nurtured, but having done what they ought in child-rearing, parents are patient to believe that despite whatever

wanderings in their child, he or she will, in the conclusion
of his or her life, if not before, return to the essential faith
and life they modeled.

Patience is needed in many areas if persons are to be
productive and mature. The point is strongly made in the
Scriptures, through examples. Noah labored for many
decades, enduring extreme ridicule, until God acted and
sent a flood. We know the story well. Abraham, having
been promised an heir, also waited for decades until the
birth of Isaac to his aged wife. At 40 years of age, Moses
waited 40 additional years for a call, and with Israel,
trekked the wilderness 40 more years in fulfilling his destiny. Job, the consummate example of patience, remained
patient in suffering—we do not know for how long.
James, in his epistle, reminded readers to emulate Job's
patience. Anyone flagging in his or her performance, anyone tempted to quit without good reason—to not finish
well—should study Job's life. The book of Job, perhaps
the oldest of the Bible library, gives to readers one of the
first lessons from Scripture—patience and perseverance.
Job practiced maturity and, in the end, was rewarded for
it.

People who are impatient fail to properly perceive God's work.
As we see in the lives of Job and others, God's timetable is
often different from our own. Much of what makes society
fail is the result of impatience. Marriages fail as much from
impatience as just about anything else. I found impatience
to be a primary contributor to problems on staff and with
students in the various colleges with which I was involved.
Certainly, impatience leads to failure in the church and
other institutions.

We live in a society obsessed with the fast track. Fast-
trackers wish to skip the time requirements and other matters necessary to cultivate opportunities, privileges and
recognition. For many years a San Francisco newspaper
recognized this trend with a special Fast Track section in
the business pages. It had news of interest to people who

wanted to make a success in life quickly without following the step-by-step process of working their way upward through the ranks.

Fast-trackers do not want to pay their dues or take their turns. They hope to take the elevator rather than the stairs to success. They do not realize that the elevator only once in a while, and quite by accident, stops at the floor of success. Some people embark on "get-rich-quick" schemes, or they negotiate for unearned recognition. They are gamblers more than users of talent and directed energy. A few make it—even chance hits it right on occasion—but they strew the wounded and slain along the way in their high risk, self-serving, family-sacrificing race to the top.

The life of Jesus stands in sharp contrast to the lives of modern-day fast-trackers. Why did Jesus wait as long as He did to launch His ministry? Certainly there were social and spiritual needs all around Him long before He started His public work. Not until Jesus was 30 years old did He begin public ministry. Even then His ministry, although exhausting and often intense, was unhurried. To have been hurried would suggest that He was not in control, that He had not started on time, that He was unprepared. But He was perfectly in control, perfectly punctual and perfectly prepared. Jesus was patient because He understood the nature of God's work.

God is not on the fast track. He seems to be leisurely. He has time to complete His purpose. Time is not major for Him. It is for us—we are mortals, suspended in time. In God's kingdom there are no real emergencies. It is good counsel: "Wait, I say, on the LORD" (Psalm 27:14, KJV). Even better for the purposes here: "Rest in the LORD, and wait patiently for him" (37:7, KJV). Patience in what we do is evidence that we believe God is in control and we are in self-control. Life is measured, divinely, by obedience to God, not by efficiency functions. Patience helps identify the mature person.

As patience is one of the compassionate marks of God, so it ought to become one of the marks of the Christian. We miss the reality that what God does we ought also to do, within reason, up to the level of our ability—no matter how modest is our attempt or performance. Isaiah captured the idea in a single verse (30:18, KJV) when he wrote: "And therefore will the LORD wait, that He may be gracious unto you. . . . Blessed are all they that wait for Him." This is to say that He is gracious to wait for us, now we will be gracious to wait for Him.

My life has been enriched with lessons about patience. Impatience is a child's attitude and emotion. When I was a child, I planted a garden. After a few days I scratched into the ground where seeds were planted and found fresh sprouts but harvested no beans later from those hills. I also dug out dark green plants that didn't look like they would grow potatoes. They were my greatest loss. My garden was lost to my impatience. My only significant crop was flowers—marigolds and asters, with only the most modest food production to present to my mother. I recall that there were several tomatoes.

A thoughtful lesson on patience sticks with me from college days. "It's too soon to quit," was the title of one of President Raymond Edman's annual sermons in Wheaton College chapel. Students who attended the college for more than one year knew they would hear that sermon every spring. Each year students would ask Edman, "When do we get 'the sermon'?" In the homily, Edman urged the students to recognize that some of them felt like dropping out, and they were about to make that decision to do so. They would later regret it if they did. He rightly urged them to continue their courses. His urging to take courage was effective, even life-changing for many students. They needed to wait out their problems.

One year I felt like quitting college. I did not have enough money to keep going. I had a wife and baby to support. There were tuitions to advance, groceries to buy, and rent to pay. There simply was not enough money. In discouragement, I went to the home of my advisor to talk with him. All I wanted on that day was his blessing and permission to drop college. He did not have any money to give me, and I didn't expect him to offer any. All he said was, "Don't quit." When I went to see my advisor at 1 p.m. I was preparing to drop out. When I left, at 2:30 p.m., I knew I would not, even though my personal circumstances were unchanged. I felt like a problem-solver, a sign of maturity.

There was resolve born in me during the conversation to press on. The only change relative to my situation occurring that day was in me. I went on to earn a bachelor's degree, a master's and a doctorate. To have quit that day would have sacrificed one of the greatest possessions of my life—my formal education. I learned an important lesson in the maturation process—be patient and stay at tasks worth doing.

One trial of Christian endurance is the delay in the promised return of Jesus Christ for His Church, a parousia promised in the Bible. The implication of Scripture is that Christians reveal failure in perception of time and God when they become impatient about Christ's return. He said He would return, and 2,000 years have intervened between the promise and the present. Where is He? Where is the promise of His coming? Even the New Testament records the question (see 2 Peter 3:4). The very implication of the question may be that Jesus did not literally mean what He said, so some theologians design exotic explanations of what that return meant or means. Some simply try to explain it away. If patience is perfected, one's faith in the return of Christ will grow strong. Paul reminded the Thessalonians to "wait for His [God's] Son from heaven" (1 Thessalonians 1:10). And he reminded the Galatians "to wait for the hope of righteousness" (5:5, KJV).

Waiting. Patience. Endurance. These are hard for us, and yet they are critical to the satisfactory finishing out of personal faith. Patience lasts all the way through to the end. Much of the Church's history focused on the lasting quality of the individual's spiritual life as evidence of genuine Christian experience. "He that endureth to the end shall be saved" (Matthew 10:22, KJV).

Patience is the quality that ties it all together. We can readily learn about vision and integrity. They are not complicated concepts, even though it takes effort to practice them effectively. But it takes one's whole life to discover whether patience can be maintained. Jesus said, "In your patience possess ye your souls" (Luke 21:19, KJV). And James wrote: "Let patience have her perfect work" (1:4, KJV). We seem to forget, if we ever knew it, that patience is a chief value in the mature Christian life. (See Romans 5:4 and 2 Peter 1:6.)

Does that mean patience is the greatest of the VIP characteristics? That is hard to say. All are needed, if we are to be VIPs. The quality we need most is the one we most lack. We do well to discover where we are weak and work on that feature. Of course, we are already VIPs (Very Important Persons) to Him—in the common meaning of VIP. We need no other evidence of our worth than the fact that God provided redemption for us. Why would God provide for the rescue of someone without worth? My goal is to live up to the imputed status, to the degree that is possible.

In our adapted meaning of VIP, I can become the man of Vision, Integrity and Patience that God means for me to become. This is the goal of my striving—to become the best person I can become. This is the person I want to be, the person I very much want to know. I wish to be not so much the person I was born biologically to be, but the one I was born spiritually to be. Biologically I will perish; spiritually I will live. My quest is to seek and become the best person I can become, and to know him before I die. But without maturity, I will never know myself well enough.

A classic illustration fits here. The story is told that the concert hall was in order for a Paderewski concert. The gleaming piano at center stage was tuned to perfection. The men and women in the audience were nearly all in their seats, and the master musician was in the wings, ready to walk on stage.

A sound, an audible gasp, went up from the audience as a child, perhaps seven or eight years of age, casually walked across the platform and sidled up on the bench. "Stop him!" came the sound of backstage voices. The mother, seeing what was happening, rushed down the aisle to retrieve her boy who, by this time, was playing chopsticks enthusiastically. But Paderewski halted the aggravated stage manager, knowing the boy would be embarrassed. At best, the scene would be clumsy. The maestro slipped into his concert jacket, formal tails, and walked out on stage behind the boy. He lifted his finger to his lips to quiet and settle the audience. He approached back of the lad who did not see him.

Stretching his left arm to the side of the keyboard, and his right to the other, the maestro made grand concert with the boy. He kept whispering to the lad as they played. When the improvisation was completed the audience erupted with applause, as Paderewski and the lad took their bows. An embarrassed, but proud, mother retrieved her wandering minstrel. "What made you keep playing?" the mother asked. "He told me," said the boy, "not to stop playing until he stopped—so I didn't stop."

I hear the instruction: "Keep going—don't stop until I stop." But I protest and feel foolish because all I can play is chopsticks. Christ turns it into a symphony. The symphony includes movements of vision, integrity and patience. The conclusion, the fourth and final movement, completes itself in maturity.

Endnotes

1 Watson, Russell, et. al. "Why He's Failing," *Newsweek*, June 4, 1990, p. 18. Copyright 1990, Newsweek, Inc. All rights reserved. Reprinted by permission.

2 Warden, Bill. "Only a Miracle," *Calgary Herald*, July 5, 1990, p. A5. Used with permission.

3 Barnes, Sandra. "National Vision Was Lost," *Calgary Herald*, July 2, 1990, p. A6.

Chapter 8

To Respond or React—
That Is the Question

*Let us run with endurance the race that is set before us,
fixing our eyes on Jesus, the author and perfecter of faith.
. . . For consider Him who has endured such hostility . . .
so that you may not grow weary and lose heart. (Hebrews
12:1-3, NASB)*

As already noted, and deserving repetition, I would very much like to meet the person I can become in full maturity. Of all persons in the world I might meet, this is the one I would choose, if limited to a single choice. One of the ways to determine the extent of my spiritual growth and maturity is to test my own and others' reactions or responses to the attitudes and conducts of my life. I would like to find at least a few of the measurements of my growth.

Growth in character and integrity is synonymous to the maturing process for Christians. Therefore, some emphasis is properly placed on process. Growth is process. The Scriptures presume that progress is the point, and maturation is an ongoing process. That maturation is directed toward perfection, a goal no one lives long enough to achieve. Spiritual maturity is sometimes translated "perfection" in the New Testament, but it does not elevate to absolute perfection for people in nature. Circumstances in people and nature forbid perfection. Spiritual maturation in life is partial manifestation of ultimate perfection. Perfection is paradise, found outside nature. Biblical sanctification, then, becomes vital to the Christian who seeks maturity.

Education, both formal and practical in experience, provides an illustration of analysis procedures. It is an interesting study to compare standard education theory with biblical. Some of the parallels are striking, as are some of the differences. Home education was a vital matter in the spiritual development of families in Israel. A major presentation commanding religious education appears in Deuteronomy chapter 6, and Jesus quoted from the same text in responding to a question about the primary commandment (Mark 12:28ff).

We presume that the maturing process can be identified and traced. Some years ago, Dr. Douglas Heath, professor of psychology at Haverford College in Pennsylvania, presented a paper entitled, "Maturing in College." Heath listed "five interdependent dimensions" to identify mature growth in a collegiate environment. We acknowledge the excellence of his theory of purpose in higher education. It will serve us simply to recite his model and focus it for our purposes. The model includes: 1) symbolization, 2) allocentrism, 3) integration, 4) stability, and 5) autonomy. With apologies to Heath for any shifting from his meanings, these words require clarification as we wish to use them. We begin by clarifying professional jargon.

1. **Symbolization** refers to the use of words, both spoken and written. Sometimes it refers to art in its various forms, including music. Any symbolic form, such as gesture, is also included to broaden the meaning of communication. Any symbolic system, useful to humanity, has some rele-

vance in maturation, in elevating humanity's conduct above animals, and the best communicators above other human beings.

In education it is presumed that as students become more effective in casting their experience into oral and written language, they are growing—processing into maturity. They will likely become more reflective people as they use symbolization processes in serious ways. They need to be aware of what they are doing. Reflection requiring language is an important preliminary to the achievement of maturation. It is more difficult to find maturity for those with less language felicity than those with more.

For the Christian, symbolization becomes sufficiently important that it is improbable that he or she will overemphasize the process. The process begins for the Christian with an orthodox perspective of Scripture. The Bible is vital to each believer so he or she is expected to read and understand it, live in the light of its truth, and communicate its message. Much of modern secular education in the West can trace its roots to those schools established for the primary reason to prepare each generation to read the Bible for its own benefit. Self-improvement and privilege as persons has been related to the ability to read, and the practice of that ability. A major effort by missionaries around the world is to assist persons to read and provide material worth reading.

The scriptural view of symbolization is an encompassing one. Believers are urged to study the Scriptures and "rightly divide them"—an impossibility to accomplish well without language felicity, and respect for the language in which the Scriptures were originally cast. This information then is recast in the language of currency for the hearer. The rhetorical use of language for sacred purposes, as noted early in First Corinthians, places the uses of language at a high level in articulating the gospel, or preaching, as "the power of God." There ought to be no doubt then that language or symbolization mastery is meaningful for Christian life and maturity. Illiterate persons have sometimes shown remarkable spiritual growth, surpassing many well-educated Christians, because they respond well to mentors who faithfully articulate what is needed from the Scriptures and other materials.

2. **Allocentrism** refers to growth away from self-centeredness "to other-centered empathy." When this is effectively done, people can see both themselves and the concerns of others through their perceptions. If they are sufficiently mature, they will act according to that growing perspective. This does not mean they will always do what others wish for them to do. By proper objectivity mature individuals become understanding, and therefore make proper judgments. They learn the right uses of tolerance and service. Allocentrism is the opposite of egocentrism.

A rising concern in the Christian for others and a decline of self-interests is key to Christian maturity. This is manifest in service to others. The concepts of service were taught and modeled by Jesus. His disciples demonstrated early resistance to it, and on occasions they simply missed the teaching.

Even Jesus' disciples, moving upward from elevation to elevation, resisted service orientation when their prejudices intervened. Not until the apostle Peter was motivated by his experience at Pentecost, and following his dream of the sheet of clean and unclean animals, did he perceive that he was to become mature in his understanding of the gospel, in part by moving away from egocentrism (most marked in modern times by narcissism) to allocentrism (best demonstrated in any generation by those who serve others with little benefit to themselves).

Altruism is vital for the practice of mature Christians. Even secular writers argue that mature persons ought to belong to "volunteer" organizations. One author contrasted the widows of the slain President Kennedy and his brother. The one retreated in tragedy to her own life and personal interests. The other turned tragedy into an opportunity for volunteer service to humankind in strong support of an organization to improve social life. If we knew enough about these persons, would we find a significant difference in the application of religious faith? Likely we would. We might also find significant personality differences that would make us reluctant to draw similar conclusions with the biographer.

3. **Integration** refers to the distinct life folded into a whole system. Children are noted for fragmenting their lives. A broken toy is everything at the moment, and perhaps for a number of days. Then it is gone and forgotten. It is not set into the fabric of the child's whole life. The child is not yet integrated.

The teacher knows his or her students are maturing when they improve their castings of relational thoughts, using better hypotheses as they move along from their freshman to senior years. If 20 years after college those students are doing even better in the integration of their thoughts, the professor can be gratified that his or her students are growing intellectually. He or she taught well. Or someone has, perhaps a parent. As adults, students worthy of the name maintain and extend education beyond classroom experience. Mature intellectual growth and ability to adapt to change is what a professor should desire from his or her class alumni. Continuing self-education relates to maturity. But many students drop the process on commencement day. They stall and will not mature intellectually as they ought.

Wholeness of life is important to the biblical concept of maturity. Christians are commanded to go on from the fundamentals of early nurture to deeper truths—both in understanding and practice. The apostle Paul acknowledged personal distress for failure of people to achieve this maturity in churches he founded. Historically, ministers have taught that Christians not only need growth to maturity, but need, to the degree possible, an evenness in growth. This evenness provides balance, and helps to avoid fanaticism.

Educators find problems of intellectual growth differentials in students. Students lacking integration may turn to alcohol, to drugs, to sex, to the occult, to dropping out. Missing in social and spiritual integration with their academics, they fill the void with whatever they stumble onto. Disillusionment often catches students. Maturity eludes them. They may even be scholarly in a chosen field, but not "whole." Teachers feel good about "maturation" in their students. Neither teachers nor students may observe it taking place in a short course. Time periods may be needed to register the effect. Christians who miss integration or wholeness also fill up the void with whatever is available, perhaps in less dramatic ways than secular humanists. The effect is the same—disillusionment, either mild or severe.

4. **Stability** refers to constructive results from new learnings, causing the person to settle into an improved pattern of doing things. Growing people are less likely to revert to former ways, ways that are unsatisfactory for effective problem-solving. Stable people can be trusted to move along with life, to work through life assignments successfully. They are strong enough to lose on occasion without being threatened or devastated by loss. They make a new try and do not abandon situations simply because they are troublesome or problematic.

Christians, as the Scriptures teach, are expected to grow into well-adjusted people. If they do not, they may backslide, jump from one congregation to another or be "tossed on waves"—sometimes angry waves. "Backsliding" is a word little used in the church in our era, but evidence of backsliding is common.

5. **Autonomy** refers to the ability of people to stand alone, if they must, and prevail in life. They have identity for themselves, passing over that which is beyond their competency, filling their lives with worthwhile experiences that they inaugurate and manage. They can stand in a minority position when circumstances indicate, because their

life integration supports the stand. They become less and less threatened as their autonomy develops. They are not unduly upset by opposition, so they can afford to be creative. They are consistent within themselves. They do not require more than modest amounts of supportive relationships.

The Christian is told to stand—"having done all, to stand" (Ephesians 6:13, KJV). Jesus and the apostles, Paul and Peter, as well as others, become magnificent historical models of mature Christians able to stand, sometimes alone, for the right against odds of whatever sort. To do so in any era requires personal maturity.

Maturity Is Seen in the Way We Respond to People

I evaluate my response to self. In responding to my person, I am responding to "people." This self-response is the most important of all human responses to human beings (the word "human" is important here). Evaluation of my inner communication with myself, or my private feelings, or my own development—all relate to the progress of maturity in me. Before God a person must be concerned about who he or she is, whereas in the world, the general population is concerned about what he or she does. Before God there must be integrity between who a person is and what he or she does. Service, based on character and motive, is the Christian pattern. We do respond to what we are. Some persons become so distressed with themselves that they end their lives in suicide. Many more are suicidal in tendency. Others sink into habits that are self-destructive. Some are pleased with their own progress so that the progress itself becomes motivation for further progress. A desire arises to perpetuate a good thing, a favorable process.

Sometimes we do not like ourselves. There are small and large things in us that we do not admire. For example, we are irritated at this or that in what we do in relationships

with other people. Rather than disregard or accept idiosyn-
crasies in others, we react negatively to them. We generally
know we are reacting, and if the irritation is with a family
member or close friend, we wonder why we do not have
enough love to feel caring. Why do we react rather than understand and help? This is common experience with husbands and wives who, inadvertently for the most part,
think in terms of win/lose with each other.

Most of us are lazy. Some of our energy is given to evading expenditure of energy. And if evasion only serves delay,
we should know we have to confront the matter at a later
time. Why not now? Why should I not say or do the appropriate thing now? Not all delay is related to patience. Why
delay the maturation experience? Momentum is good and,
as we know, an object in motion tends to remain in motion. Life is very different for those who accept themselves
than it is for those who do not. Different even though
everything around both groups is similar, even the same.

What can I *do* if God is with me? For the believer there
is an unbroken line drawn from Abraham, nearly 4,000
years ago to the present. Much of the Scripture is cast to inform readers that God is with His children, caring for
them, sustaining them, nurturing them. The problem
seems to be that those children are often unwilling to be
obedient to the level that God requires if His resources are
to be committed to them. They can do whatever they are
supposed to do. Moses alerted Israel on obedience: "what I
am commanding you today is not too difficult for you or
beyond your reach. It is not up in heaven. . . . Nor is it beyond the sea. . . . [T]he word is very near you; it is in your
mouth and in your heart so you may obey it" (Deuteronomy 30:11-14).

What can I *be* if God is with me? This question only
seems easier than the one above relative to conduct. Scripture seems clear to us and more readily applied on matters
of conduct in relation to our souls and spirits. Only our resistance to biblical injunction prevents us from developing

the spiritual mind. If we achieve the spiritual mind-set our practical problem becomes the application of our better being to better doing. When our conduct fails, it is commonly due to lapse from our advances in *being*. We must follow Christian conduct with devotion and care if integration is to occur. We begin to realize that what we do is what we are.

We evaluate our response to others. Writers have discussed the "vein of meanness" in young businesspeople on the fast track, in entertainers clawing their way to high career positions, in politicians who dedicate themselves to win elections at any cost, and in athletes who gain recognition by defeating others any way they can. Persons who think and function in these ways may be incapable of responding effectively to themselves or others.

We rightly challenge persons who find the "real sensitive man" underneath the "hard operator" on Wall Street or the business station, or in the church hierarchy. Some men and women have the ability to compartmentalize their lives, dividing their responses according to their situations. We know that even murderous Mafia men are generally dutiful family members. It is understood that women, even of offending families, are not to be objects of violence and murder. We admire that degree of humane respect, but deplore the loss of wholeness in Mafia men. If they murder only "enemy" men they are no less murderers.

When persons analyze their disagreeable confrontations, they should begin with their own part in those exchanges. What did they do? What did they say? Do they generally act and communicate in this pattern? The ultimate question is: did they respond to solve a problem or to react? A response intent upon problem-solving has healing and solution in it. A reaction, in the way the word is used here, generally exacerbates an already difficult situation. Self-analysts can evaluate how and when others respond or react to them. They will never please some persons. Others they will please for a time, and later lose. Still others they will not please at first, but later these others become disciples. Often these last become their strongest and most lasting supporters. We can learn much about ourselves and others by evaluating changing responses in ourselves and in them.

Maturity Is Seen in the
Way We Respond to Problems

We ought to evaluate our response to large problems. It is not always agreed what constitutes a large problem for each person—a death in the family, a divorce, the loss of a job, or a move from one neighborhood to another. It is generally agreed that these are significant issues in one's life and require large personal resources to meet them and prevail. What is a problem if it is not an opportunity, or an opportunity if it is not a problem? Those persons who "affirmatively image" their lives are not, as a rule, offended at problems, but turn them into opportunities. And opportunities provide some of the reason for living. There is excitement in them.

Money management is a significant problem many families will encounter, and it commonly overwhelms them. For others, budgeting is treated as matter-of-factly as any issue in their lives. They are mature in their use of money. They figure income and costs and live within the boundaries of their formulas. They do not fight the facts. Much can be learned about a person in his or her treatment of personal financial obligations. There are various reasons why people do not pay their bills—poverty, miserliness, irresponsibility. It is likely that irresponsibility is larger than the lack of funds. Money issues are more often related to maturity development than they are to morality or general circumstances.

One way we discover irresponsibility is to perceive our neglect. We fail to do necessary detail work. To take time to address an envelope, write a check, and keep records seems too demanding for some of us. To avoid important detail work is a sign of immaturity. Failure to do detail work is generally seen in various omissions: delaying household chores, disregarding mail that begs for reply, permitting unfinished tasks to accumulate, postponing any duty that does not compel immediate action, and overlooking other matters making a difference in life. So families do not have their needs met, and jobs are haphazardly done. Social services, presumed to exist to solve human problems, are often not well designed or carried through. I discovered in my own professional life not to expect excellence in getting the humdrum things done, and when chores are taken on they are sometimes completed at the deadline, usually after, seldom earlier.

One is forced to lower human expectations. Currently the situations seem to be worse than they formerly were. The modern development of precise machinery and electronic gadgets makes the casual human being appear even less competent than when technology was undeveloped. We need not learn to spell words because electronic typewriters store words correctly spelled. Why learn how to spell? The tendency of the period is to search for a machine to make up for human omission. In a request to have a small typing job done in two offices with secretarial pools, I found no one who felt they could venture the project.

We ought also to evaluate our response to small problems. The small aggravations appear to accumulate for us, wearing us down. For example, the modern family seems to be so fragile that marriages may be deemed unacceptable, therefore divorced because of "irreconcilable differences." Seldom are there truly irreconcilable differences, but there are irreconcilable persons who refuse change. There may be different political viewpoints, different tastes in music, different attitudes about a pet, different sleep and work schedules, different feelings about anything—and many accept these and similar excuses as substantive for breaking up a family. In most instances in counseling sessions, I discovered one or both parties did not attempt seriously to reconcile differences.

Lack of maturity in husbands and wives must be a major cause, if not the major cause, for marriage breakup. However, the blame is put on lack of communications, money mismanagement, intimacy differentials, general imperfections in mates. If focus can be made on what is mature conduct, and then translated to specific problems, a marriage will improve. Nearly all happily married couples survived their excuses. They matured.

Never has so much assistance been available as there is today for virtually any problem. Significant manpower is devoted to helping family members, even their pets, to solve problems, or better yet, to avoid them through preventive means. For example, premarital counseling was virtually unknown prior to World War II. It never occurred to my parents to seek counseling before their marriage in 1922. Nor did my wife and I, both Christians, think of seeking counsel in 1943 when we were married. In our more than 50 years together we remain happily married and belong to a generation that has a more successful record of marriage than the generations that followed, generations receiving more help than we did for family life.

There may be reason to believe that the materials premaritals read and the counseling they received raised expectations which, when unmet, became, on occasion, cause for breakup. Therapists are frustrated with counseling couples and getting negative results. Consider, for example, the book *We've Had One Hundred Years of Psychotherapy and the World's Getting Worse* by James Hillman and Michael Ventura (Harper Collins, 1992).

Marriage breakdown for younger men and women is occurring despite marriage counseling and assistance from health and social services, larger and more easily available recreational privileges, higher standards of living, and increase in both formal and informal education. All these and more were designed to provide the "better life." At the turn of the 20th century about one percent of American youths attended college. As we approach the end of the 20th century, the percentage receiving at least some education on the collegiate level is about half the population. Many observers have openly questioned the benefits of college education for at least half of those. That half appear not to be improved by higher education. But, in a free society, the right to seek education belongs to all who wish to seek it. The question arises: For what purpose? How does formal education help in practical living? Does counseling?

It is sometimes argued that formal education increases stress for some students who not only educate their minds, but develop their skills to earn more money and be found in the power arenas of society. We seem unable to take as much duty and hardship as our forebears—or the nature of hardship has changed. Perhaps comparisons or contrasts are inappropriate. The "hardships" may have changed or escape hatches been provided. Divorce, formerly used sparingly but available, is currently popular for escape from marriage.

We are told that many students are distraught at having to take school examinations, that headaches and other stress problems are increasing. We may be in a similar situation as that of a bird of prey, or even a lion or tiger, born and raised in a protected environment, therefore rendered incapable of functioning in normal habitat. Released into the fields of the world a coddled generation may perish. Writing about the stress connection between mind and body, Richard Saltus stated:

> When some employees of Western Electric Co. were challenged by difficult video games or mental math tests, their blood pressure and heart rate shot up as if their very lives were in danger. According to stress researcher, Dr. Robert Eliot, it may well be true. In his laboratory at the University of Nebraska at Omaha, he found that certain people react to minor aggravations with biological responses as obsolete as

stone axes. He called them "hot reactors" and
believed their behavior can make them abnor-
mally prone to sudden death from heart attacks.
Such a reaction may have made sense in the face
of a saber-toothed tiger, Eliot says, "but in the
modern world, it's physiological foolishness."[1]

In research on stress, it has been found that some people
thrive on stress and pressure. They need it to achieve goals
in their lives. The researchers are trying to find what factors make up this "hardiness." Why, for example, did medics helping badly wounded men while under heavy fire in
Vietnam suffer less stress than men in North America who
were in training to become medics?

During December 1983, a group of researchers not ori-
ented to the church found that marriages of "churchgoers"
were more effective ("48% more effective") than those of
nonchurchgoers. They added, at the time of the publication of their results, that "we do not know the reasons for
this phenomenon." How could churchgoers be so much
more effective? The researchers were surprised, genuinely
surprised, at their findings. If they believed in a personal
God, would they be surprised? Possibly. But the surprise
would be a different one—that the marriages were not even
better than they were found to be. A 48 percent more effective result is not sufficiently better, if all respondents were
serious about the meaning of the church and a personal experience with God.

Apparently the researchers were unwilling to say that
perhaps God, whether actually God or because of believer's
illusion, did make a difference in lives. It appears that persons who believe in God, and find some expression of that
belief in faithful church attendance, develop better processes for life. In much of secular critical writing the assertion is the opposite—that the believer is "weak-minded" in
God-dependence rather than "strong-minded" in self-de-
pendence. This would be a worthy research project which,

although treated by graduate psychology researchers, needs a fresh look by competent Christian scholars.

Generally, research has shown that individuals are benefited in their lives by church and faith orientations. Even "faith-in-God" believers may not recognize that their added resources come from spiritual life. As noted in an earlier chapter, the Bible includes an emphasis on "endurance." One is rightly concerned that so much is said today about "stress" and so little about "hardiness" or "endurance." Mature persons find ways of balancing stress with hardiness, and so prevail.

A study of the views of religious men and women reported results that were, again, opposite of what the researchers expected. Sheena Sethi of Stanford University and Martin Seligman of the University of Pennsylvania, according to Marilyn Elias reporting in *USA Today*, found that "[m]ost optimistic were fundamentalists; least, liberal religions. Most pessimistic of all: the one-third of Unitarians who didn't believe in God." Elias reported that "[f]ollowers of that 'old time religion,' a favorite target of comics, may have the last laugh: Their faith gives them a strong mental health edge." Elias quoted Sethi: "We know optimistic people are less vulnerable to depression, and optimism correlates with high achievement. . . . [W]hat we found was exactly the opposite of what we expected."[2]

Other research supportive of applied faith to life, to conduct, to marriage and the family is usually passed over by a humanistic professional body of counselors and analysts. Even more problematic are their beliefs and practices which are contrary to a growing research showing positive results related to faith in God as applied to daily conduct. For example, it was discovered that persons who say grace at their meals are healthier than those who do not. The researchers believed that this was due to relaxation caused by the delay to pray. They did not propose that, indeed, God may bless food. Prayer inadvertently caused persons to avoid "bolting" their food.

Maturity Is Seen in the Way We Respond to Pressures

We evaluate our responses to short-range pressures. What happens to celebrities—athletes, for example? If an athlete gains the height of achievement in his or her sport, receives excessive adulation for a period of time, earns the highest income he or she will ever receive in life before he or she is 35 years of age and is nearly forgotten by the madding crowd for the last half of his or her life, he or she is a candidate for personal tragedy. The high expectations for him or her to perform well in a season, even in a single game, may test him or her beyond his or her ability to manage pressure.

Without sufficient personal resources, the sports figure or other celebrity may turn to drugs or alcohol—or even, for the need of money, lend his or her name to nefarious causes. The problem has, in fact, become sufficiently large that several major sports organizations address the issue of orientation to create a more mature approach to life by athletes and to prepare them for reentry into a world without hero-worship, fawning publicists, high income and social privilege.

Fantasy about stress may create stress. Does the very implication that we cannot manage stress *create* stress? One cause of stress is the anticipation or expectation of stress. People are naive if they believe they can escape stress. It is plentiful and available for all and must be faced. Nevertheless, it appears that we are effective in creating much of our own stress sometimes because of the poor management that leads to it. There is a compounding process at work.

To experience stress may be taken as a badge of courage and prelude to success. Persons in influential positions are supposed to be busy, making difficult decisions, and becoming recognizable in general society. They are presumed to be on a track that takes them to higher levels of performance and experience than common folk. And this participation is presumed to create stress. For some persons, not to experience stress is not to experience esteem.

Stress in a person may put him or her in league with the "right" people. Among celebrities, or alleged celebrities, it is common to discuss openly their experiences, even encounters, with their psychiatrists. It is presumed in conversation between celebrities that they have personal psychiatrists. It is an "in" thing in some circles to meet regularly with a shrink. And some of these sessions go on for many years. We have only scattered evidence about the results of the fad—some favorable, some unfavorable. Many celebrities, while crediting their counselors with supportive assistance, nevertheless appear incompetent to manage their lives, assignments and families. We do know that many persons in pressured occupations do not encounter great stress, while many in less pressurized situations do. This might be accounted for in the differences in hardiness in the groups.

What do we need in order to learn how to cope with changes in life? Changes, whether perceived as good or ill, have much to do with stimulating human stress responses. In the interplay of factors we seem to release or inhibit some of the chemical processes of our bodies. Chemical changes affect our physiology and psychology. And, we are told, there are also genetic forces at work. We are also told, by critics, that genetics are "a myth." Genetic influences in each person appear to be mixed between strong and weak and in-between. We are likely vulnerable to this or that disease, this or that circumstance, especially where we are weak. In other factors, we inherit strength. The several influences complicate the management of our lives. Mature persons will not fall back upon genetics or chemistry to justify unsatisfactory conduct.

Researchers suggest stress plays upon physical weaknesses in persons. Stress, if we permit it, is a strong soldier preparing attack at weak points. Persons vulnerable to stress often claim that they have visceral pains, headaches, chest pains, allergies and other physical problems that are not traceable in them to physical causes. In many of the cases studied, the problems were related to minor aggravations. The cause of stress in most instances was not life-threatening. But the stressful person may feel life is in mysterious danger. Numbers of stress-inducing experiences seem to be breakdowns in basic interpersonal relationships—like the inability to get along well with others, at home or at work.

Rather high percentages of the general population seem not to have been prepared to cope with real life. Repeated failure with life leads to demoralization. This inability to cope, or lack of preparedness, becomes particularly embarrassing for Christians who, presumably, are provided with spiritual resources that can help them manage otherwise stressful lives. What happens when Christians pray? What happens when they are nourished from the Scriptures? What happens when they meditate, when they "think on these things"? What happens when they put learnings into practice? Good things ought to come out of such exercises, but for many, personal equilibrium is elusive.

Observers generally agree that Christians, as community, seem not to apply as effectively as they should what they claim to believe. While taking a course in medieval history at the University of Washington, I was impressed by the number of times class members and the professor were forced to talk about Christianity. One cannot treat history competently in the Western world at any time during the last 2,000 years without some knowledge of the impact of Christianity. The professor, well-educated and Jewish in background, maintained a personal secular opinion of life and history. He was an avowed humanist.

However, the professor paused at an important juncture one day when a negative remark in class focused on Christianity in Europe in 1300. As an historian, he said, he wanted the class to know that Christianity had not been widely tried in Europe in the way the Bible described the faith and the involvement of Christ. That although the people called them-

selves Christians, he argued, they retained many pagan practices and often gave an unsatisfactory impression of Christianity. He openly expressed the hope to the class that the
members would not equate Christianity with the conduct of
many of the people who espoused it, either in the days before
the Renaissance or since. Christianity was, he believed, purer
than Christians in their conduct represented it. To discuss
Christianity he rightly urged the class to differentiate, where
they needed to do so, the teachings of Christ from the conduct
of Christians and the Church.

We evaluate our responses to long-range pressures. In giving attention to new communication media, society at large
seems to have generated its own trauma over such matters as
atomic warfare, shaky economics, family failure, weight control, old age, death and several scores of other issues. But what
are the issues that divide persons, that hurt families and communities, that lead to breakdown between cultures and nations? By and large, the population devotes its time to
relatively unimportant matters, and the power brokers managing the engines of the world know that. Most studies show
that common people, at large, are taken up with personal current concerns: their health, their jobs, their homes, their children. Thus far there is little evidence that fear of national
enemies, fear of atomic fallout, fear of depletion in resources,
fear of environmental pollution or fear of other massive world
problems has much influence over how people live or think.
There are theories that the great unresolved problems create
deleterious effects that are not easily measured because most
persons do not report related responses faithfully. But that
there are negative effects touching personal lives, effects that
create malaise, is widely believed.

How do men and women treat unseen and unknown effects, such as mysterious stresses, in their lives? For some
there is flight. They do not listen to the news, do not travel
beyond the resident community, do not even vote. This
conduct treats issues with an isolation of self and sometimes including the few others with whom these persons

have to do. Some stab at various "solutions" and never quite integrate their lives. Others treat troublesome issues directly and do what they can to improve matters. They are the mature citizens in the populations.

At this juncture in history there has intensified bizarre approaches to human problems and concerns. We will refer here to just one, but there are many. They do not qualify as mature solutions. There is the well-known and strange case of Bishop James A. Pike. That Pike possessed intellectual prowess, there is no doubt. He gained attention and approval from numerous persons with proper academic credentials. He was masterful in oral presentation of a thesis. I once heard him present a case that was a rhetorical masterpiece in an auditorium before a thousand persons. He had been educated for the law, but turned to pastoral ministry. He became vicar of the Cathedral of St. John the Divine in New York City where he made an eminent reputation for himself. Elected the Episcopal Bishop of California, he moved to San Francisco. Controversy, from which in one form or other he had never been free, intensified around Pike. Resigning as Bishop, he became one of the senior members, with Robert Maynard Hutchins, the eminent former president of the University of Chicago, of a think tank in Santa Barbara, California. In 1971 he lost his life in a remote desert area of Palestine as he was tracing the wilderness journeys of Jesus. One might presume that Pike would be a mature man, a model for other men. He claimed to be a liberal Christian.

From the time Pike entered church ministry he moved away from orthodoxy. He did not begin from a strong orthodox position anyway. He early rejected biblical views like the virgin birth and theology of the Trinity. His gravitation into a secularized religious perception led to tension between himself and other clergy even in his denomination. As he grew older, he seemed less and less what he was expected to be in a clerical role. He became more and more controversial in areas in which he was expected to show clear leadership.

Married three times, Pike incurred the wrath of the California Episcopal authorities when he made little or no effort to gain approval for his second divorce and third marriage. His son committed suicide, an event that personally rocked Pike as nothing else had done. He began to openly explore the occult. In a well-known 1967 seance, Pike seemed taken by the work of the Rev. Arthur Ford, a prominent medium who was also a Disciples of Christ minister. In the seance, broadcast by the Canadian Television Network, Ford claimed to bring Pike and his dead son together. Other deceased persons, known to Pike, were also presumably brought into the conversation. Critics watching the program believed that Pike was somehow gulled by Ford. Pike believed the seance was genuine. Listeners were divided on what they heard.

After the deaths of Ford and Pike, Allen Spragget, the Canadian journalist who introduced Pike to Ford, acknowledged Ford's careful pre-seance research into Pike's personal life. The research materials were made public. When compared with Ford's dramatic responses on the television tape, the presentation appears to have been staged. Pike, unable to accept biblical materials, with historical support, was persuaded by the trickery of a clever medium. Educated to demand, recognize and respond to evidence, Pike was impressed by a gracious charlatan, but a charlatan nonetheless.

During recent years other intellectuals, rejecting biblical revelation, have been caught up in occult or bizarre ideas and exercises. Carl Rogers, the eminent psychologist, apparently gave some support to contacting the dead. Dr. Elisabeth Kubler-Ross, the eminent student of death and dying, followed something similar to Rogers in her preoccupation with life's ending. How much easier it ought to be to accept the revelation of the Scriptures about life and endings.

Still another type of reaction to problems is to make oneself the center of the universe. Some years ago a new pattern of songs began to appear on the popularity charts. The songs captured some of the new narcissism of self-adulation that emerged in America after the student expressions of the 1960s. These songs might be represented by the popular title of a Frank Sinatra hit, written by Paul Anka, entitled "My Way." The lyrics accented the general concept that one is independent and may do whatever he or she wishes, in an attitude suggesting bravery and spunk. There is, when one perceives the approach, large arrogance in this self-process.

A great danger, of course, is to believe that when one regards rugged individualism a matter of admirable strength and appears in old age to have prevailed, that person has found safety. This is simply untrue. Captain Ahab chasing the white whale is no more in his death than the dying man who fears his shadow. And Timothy Leary, who espoused "turning on" to the drug culture as well as "dropping out" from the old culture after World War II argued for creative dying when he learned he had fatal prostate cancer. One wonders if these persons are like the lad who whistles while passing the graveyard as night falls.

A large lesson one day in my high school sophomore literature class was the meaning of a poem, a poem we were commissioned to memorize together with "Flower in the Crannied Wall." (To understand the flower was to understand God.) It gave the same general impression back then as Anka's "My Way" song may do in current society. So we spent the hour with "Invictus" by William Ernest Henley who argued for his "unconquerable soul." He seemed, even from mute pages, to shout, "I am the master of my fate, I am the captain of my soul." But on another day, we found Tennyson took a different view, rejecting any "moaning of the bar" in his putting out to sea. Why not? His answer: "I hope to meet my Pilot face to face, When I have crossed the bar."

Each person must ultimately conclude, even if he or she is less influential to others than a popular entertainer, whether he or she will do things his or her way or God's way. To do them my own way is a reaction; to do them

God's way is a response. Arrogance and wisdom, even if not perceived, are at odds here.

Persons must be at their best in responding to someone higher than themselves. If they were righteous enough—that is to say, perfect—they could well respond with confidence in their own creativity. But they are not in so enviable a position. Nevertheless, they can cultivate better selves through progressively improved knowledge, conduct and attitudes. These are most easily felt and observed in love, peace, joy, patience, courage, hope, problem-solving, service, humility and wisdom, which is, in summary, reliance upon the biblical Word applied in life.

Tests for maturity tend to relate to the ways individuals respond to people (relationships), to problems (events), to pressures (feelings). Those who cultivate relationships with a sense of service, love, patience and respect are growing in maturity. Those who solve problems through practical conduct, beliefs and attitudes are growing in maturity. Those who meet stress with intelligence, peace and wholeness are growing in maturity. Maturity is our word, our goal.

Our purpose here has been to identify maturity, principally Christian maturity. Finding what Christian maturity is, we argue that it is the personal elevated status all Christians should seek. A mature Christian not only follows Christ in spiritual growth, but rightly finds satisfaction in his or her own development as a Christian. The mature Christian is thoroughly furnished unto every good work, and the first work is him or herself. One's objective ought to be to become the best person he or she can become. When the person approaches that potential, he or she is mature. I would like to meet that person.

Endnotes

1 Saltus, Richard. "Mind and Body," *San Francisco Examiner,* August 14, 1983, p. A-1.

2 Ellis, Marilyn. "Strict religious faith lifts mind as well as spirit," *USA Today*, August 2, 1993, p. 1-A. Copyright 1993, USA Today. Reprinted with permission.

Appendix

Words or Ideas Used in the Bible to Characterize Mature Christians:

1. Brotherly kindness
2. Endurance
3. Faith
4. Forbearance
5. Forgiveness
6. Gentleness
7. Gifts
8. Godliness
9. Goodness
10. Growth
11. Holiness
12. Hope
13. Humility
14. Impartiality
15. Integrity
16. Joy
17. Knowledge
18. Longsuffering
19. Love
20. Meekness
21. Mercy
22. Patience
23. Peace
24. Perseverance
25. Prayer
26. Problem-solving
27. Purity
28. Quietness
29. Service
30. Temperance
31. Understanding
32. Unity
33. Virtue
34. Wholeness

Words or Ideas Used in the Bible to Characterize the Opposite:

1. Adultery
2. Anger
3. Blasphemy
4. Carnality
5. Conformation to the world
6. Covetousness
7. Evil
8. Filthy communication
9. Fornication
10. Haughtiness
11. Hypocrisy
12. Inordinate affection
13. Jealousy
14. Lasciviousness
15. Lying
16. Malice
17. Reaction
18. Revenge
19. Uncleanness
20. Wrath